PHYSICAL EDUCATION TIPS FROM THE TRENCHES

Charmain Sutherland

HUMAN KINETICS

Library of Congress Cataloging-in-Publication Data

Sutherland, Charmain, 1966-
    Physical education tips from the trenches / by Charmain Sutherland.
        p. cm.
    Includes bibliographical references.
    ISBN 0-7360-3709-8
    1. Physical education and training--Study and teaching (Elementary) 2. Physical
    education and training--Study and teaching (Middle school) I. Title.

    GV363 .S88 2001
    613.7'07'1--dc21   2001026460

ISBN: 0-7360-3709-8

Acquisitions Editor: Scott Wikgren; **Developmental Editor:** Myles Schrag; **Assistant
Editors:** Lee Alexander, Jennifer L. Davis, Amanda S. Ewing, J. Gordon Wilson; **Copyeditor:**
Jennifer M. Thompson; **Proofreader:** Kathy Bennett; **Graphic Designer:** Stuart Cartwright;
Graphic Artist: Yvonne Griffith; **Cover Designer:** Jack W. Davis; **Art Manager:** Craig
Newsom; **Illustrator (interior and cover art):** Dick Flood; **Printer:** Versa Press

Printed in the United States of America   10   9   8   7   6   5   4   3   2   1

Human Kinetics
Web site: www.humankinetics.com

United States: Human Kinetics
P.O. Box 5076
Champaign, IL 61825-5076
800-747-4457
e-mail: humank@hkusa.com

Canada: Human Kinetics
475 Devonshire Road Unit 100
Windsor, ON N8Y 2L5
800-465-7301 (in Canada only)
e-mail: orders@hkcanada.com

Europe: Human Kinetics
Units C2/C3 Wira Business Park
West Park Ring Road
Leeds LS16 6EB, United Kingdom
+44 (0) 113 278 1708
e-mail: humank@hkeurope.com

Australia: Human Kinetics
57A Price Avenue
Lower Mitcham, South Australia 5062
08 8277 1555
e-mail: liahka@senet.com.au

New Zealand: Human Kinetics
P.O. Box 105-231, Auckland Central
09-523-3462
e-mail: hkp@ihug.co.nz

To my loved ones

CONTENTS

PREFACE

Have you ever gone to work and had everything go as you planned? Probably not. Unpredictability is the norm in teaching, and it is certainly the norm in teaching physical education. The job is difficult. You work in heat, cold, and wind; and sometimes you get caught in the rain. Your best-laid plans are ruined by an all-day talent show. A mother fears her daughter will get hurt if she participates in physical education class. A fellow teacher wants to punish her student by taking away his physical education time. You've got more obstacles than a postal worker, yet dozens if not hundreds of students expect you to deliver daily.

These obstacles are hard to overcome, but take heart: the guide you are about to read was designed to help you do just that. *Physical Education Tips from the Trenches* is a resource created with you in mind—a conscientious, dedicated, caring teacher: the quality physical education teacher. This book provides commonsense advice that will help you take on the endless supply of unexpected challenges and effectively deal with them. Quality physical education teachers are in demand because they are committed to providing the best physical experiences for their students, accompanied by dedication to the whole educational process.

Quality physical education teachers do have sense, you know. They can make sense out of the many obstacles in their way. Even more important, they can overcome those obstacles to ensure that class time makes sense to the many children who count on their physical education teacher. If you are new to the profession of physical education teaching, you will discover, in this sympathetic guide, more than 80 real-life events that could happen to you. If you are an experienced teacher, they probably already have happened.

As this handy book shows, you are not alone. Many stellar and committed elementary and middle school physical education teachers are serious about helping their students succeed and are flexible and sharp enough to make it happen. By offering these real-life occurrences and some solutions for dealing with them, I hope that rookie and veteran teachers alike will be able to make sense out of the insane and laugh at situations that otherwise might be infuriating. Maybe you will even uncover a better physical education lesson than the one that was ruined by an unexpected problem. If all of these examples already have happened to you, then you can enjoy the read and reminisce about situations that make physical education both fun and challenging.

These challenges are our responsibility—the responsibility of quality physical education teachers, that is. This book is for the ones who take their roles seriously and don't allow false stereotypes of physical education teachers to live on in their communities. That is the bulk of us, who believe that teaching physical education is the greatest job in the world!

This book introduces more than 80 types of situations that unexpectedly occur in a physical education teacher's life, followed by advice on how to deal with these situations. After witnessing some teaching methods I didn't agree with and struggling through several foul-ups of my own, I thought a guide could rescue others who will face these same obstacles. Each situation in this book concludes with a real-life story that sheds additional light on the problem—either what went wrong for a teacher who made a common mistake, or what went right for a teacher who used an acceptable solution to the problem. Here is the easy-to-follow format you will find for each situation in the book:

- "Obstacle": What is the basic problem caused by the situation at hand?

- "Common Mistakes": These are possible actions that many physical education teachers might take without thoroughly considering the problem. Often, we act hastily or angrily, or take the other extreme and don't act when it is our duty to do so.

- "Solutions": These are ways to hurdle over the obstacle using common sense. They will help you avoid the temptation of being lured into acting too rashly or not at all.

- "Tips": These are ideas to help make sure the obstacle doesn't occur in the first place, or at least decrease its size or chip away at it one step at a time.

- "Real-Life Story": A true tale should help you remember that you are not alone. Others have experienced similar situations and lived to tell about them.

Each situation in the book is easily organized using the preceding categories. These situations are presented in a fun, lighthearted way, but they also contain a sincere purpose. As you go through the book, note the obstacles you have faced or can expect to face. Consider what mistakes you want to avoid, and what commonsense solutions and tips might help you do so. Finally, in each situation presented, read how a teacher's real-life story occurred and envision how your own real-life story might turn out.

Also make sure to look at the appendixes in the back of the book, where you can find physical education proverbs and sayings and a physical education dictionary. As a professional in physical education, you will be reminded again that kids say the "darnedest things" and they spice up your days in ways you never imagine when you get out of bed each morning.

If you ever needed support on the physical education playing field or in the gym, you are now holding it in your hands. If you ever needed someone to share your frustrations with, you now have thousands of physical education colleagues who understand the tough times. Read this book as a crisis arises, or all at once to be prepared for any situation. Of course, you also can read it just for enjoyment. This can be your guide, your reference book, and perhaps it will offer a little bit of sanity to your unpredictable, challenging, yet ultimately rewarding career in physical education.

INTRODUCTION

PHYSICAL EDUCATION IN THE 21st CENTURY

The students stroll into the school building, following their same route to their classroom, as always, ho hum. There's math, then reading, science, and finally their favorite time of the day. Hooray, it's physical education time! For those students who don't have physical education until the end of the day, it's like waiting a lifetime for a chance to get to PE class.

Physical education class is almost every student's favorite class. It's the coolest class of the day. It's the chance for freedom from the students' chairs, books, and papers. They laugh, holler, shout, play, run, chase, jump, release, and have fun. That's the attitude most of the students have about physical education class.

You want the students to feel this way about your class. When you get them to love coming to physical education class, that's when you really can teach them. Their desires are so strong to participate in physical education that they pay attention, follow directions, grasp information, and learn while enjoying what they are doing.

Not only are the students watching the hands of the clock as it climbs to physical education time, the classroom teacher also is checking her watch for that chance for a break. The classroom teacher loves PE time because it means a break from the students for 45 minutes. Then, when the students come back from physical education, they have worked out, released some energy, and are ready to settle down.

Physical education time is an opportunity for students to finally look at one another, talk to one another, and speak in more than a whisper. You know how it feels to stretch your muscles after sitting in a long meeting—it feels good. That's how the students feel when the teacher says, "Let's line up for PE."

Physical education teachers are more than just "jocks." Our responsibilities are many. We must make lesson plans and stay organized enough to teach all the students in our schools while also being prepared for injuries and many elements outside of our control.

Still, teaching physical education is a great job. Is there anyone else you would want to trade jobs with? Going to work every day is a gift!

The challenges that arise while performing this job are all unexpected surprises and also should be treated as gifts. Each day we open up a new experience that will make us laugh or help us to handle a surprise better the next time a similar experience comes along.

The public will always have their opinions about the worth of physical education and the abilities of physical education teachers. It's our job to change negative perceptions and prove the skeptics of physical education wrong through good lessons, good results, and positive outcomes. Those of us who teach this type of physical education can make the difference. We know that teachers of quality physical education are the genuine PE teachers and actually have as much, if not more, sense than most other professionals. We have to. Look at what we have to do each day.

So, What Do You Do for a Living?

You meet someone and he asks, "So, what do you do for a living?" You can read the expression on his face when you say, "Teach PE." Sometimes you feel as if you must defend your occupation, explaining that teaching physical education is so great because of how much you love what you do. Reactions you get may include the following: "Oh, how fun." "That's easy." "That's not really a job." "You're lucky." Or, "Cool."

People don't know that the quality physical education teacher's job consists of 360 minutes of on-the-go, nonstop supervising, managing, teaching, nursing, counseling, helping, refereeing, modifying, talking, encouraging, walking, withstanding the weather, and coaching. Our job has a little bit of everything. We do the jobs of a store manager, clerk, nurse, counselor, mother, father, referee, speaker, coach, party coordinator, entertainer, hairdresser, custodian, physical therapist, weatherperson, fund-raiser, promoter, director, lawyer, and police officer.

Compare the physical education teacher's job to others . . .

Job title/description	Done in physical education?
The clerk must stand all day	Yes
The counselor hears about problems	Yes
The doctor advises about medical conditions	Yes
The weatherperson listens to complaints about the weather	Yes
The lawyer hears complaints and threats	Yes
The construction worker does manual labor	Yes
The retail worker must sell the product enthusiastically	Yes

What's not to love about our job? We don't have to wear ties with our shirts. We don't have to squeeze, pull, or wiggle into hose and spend the day adjusting them. We dress comfortably, in order to do a job that is meaningful, important, interesting, and fun. Since we have a job that most people do as a hobby, we do play as we work. How great it is to teach a hobby or sport that you love yourself!

Sure, there are "those days," but in the long run, what physical education teachers do for a living makes a difference and the quality PE teacher loves doing it.

Professional Play Teacher

Doctors, lawyers, accountants, and business people are considered professionals in the job world. So are classroom teachers. However, physical education teachers are not always considered professionals. Even if a PE teacher is called a "physical education specialist," "fitness instructor," or "specialized universal physical fitness expert," the term "physical education teacher" doesn't always get professional status.

Don't let that taint your teaching, your dreams, or your aspirations; just allow that thought to be your driving force to prove your professionalism. "Play teacher," "games teacher," "the gym teacher," "coach"—whatever the label, you know that you are a professional at what you do.

This reputation as the professional play teacher rather than a bona fide teacher of a valuable subject (physical education) may occur because some physical education teachers incorrectly show others in the world that all we do is play. "Here, kids, here's the ball, now go play. No fighting." Our job is far more than playing kickball and dodgeball. Good physical education practices are found in the gyms of quality physical education teachers.

Your only way out of this "professional play teacher" trap is to prove the skeptics wrong. Make every day a day of proof that your subject is worthwhile! Sure, you teach skills through play and games, but the learning comes first and the play reinforces the skill. If other professionals would make learning fun through play and games, work wouldn't be as dull and people would enjoy learning and working as we do.

The Athletic Shoe Doesn't Always Fit

You've heard the saying, "If the shoe fits, wear it." Well, in this case, the athletic shoe doesn't always fit as people assume it would. Not all physical education teachers wear the same athletic shoes. All of us involved with physical education, athletics, sports, and recreation have personalities, interests, and skills that come from many different shoe boxes.

All physical education teachers are unique. Some like to run and some don't, some are loud and some aren't, some are giants and some are petite. However, all physical educators need to have the same genuine desire to help students want to be physically active and healthy for a lifetime.

Physical education has proven to attract a wide variety of people who teach this incredible subject. Some are fitness fanatics. Some are just fit. Some know how to be fit but are not.

Some teachers coach after their job, and some have interests far removed from the games venue.

If you are good at your job, the principal may ask you to do projects around the school. Many physical education teachers are good at the following things, which are common demands of teaching physical education classes and the situations we have to face:

- Handling crowds
- Getting students motivated

- Selling and promoting items
- Being flexible
- Organizing big events
- Handling crises

Sometimes your physical education class will be singing and preparing for the spring musical. Sometimes your class might be spent in an assembly. You might be asked to work the telephones in the office for various reasons. Many times your class will not be physical education related at all, but it will become your duty to do what the principal asks you to do. You might be asked to run the office, run errands, deliver things, cover a class for a sick classroom teacher, or work as the nurse.

The quality physical education teachers do jobs for the school, the children, the principal, and society. Wearing many hats comes with the territory. The physical education teacher is also the one who wears the nurse's hat, the mother's and father's hat, the police officer's hat, the ringmaster's hat, the cheerleader's hat, and so many others.

Athletic shoes are worn by many physical education teachers, but the same shoe does not fit all those teachers. They are as individual and unique as other professionals. The quality physical education teacher has a closet full of different hats and shoes and wears them well, no matter what the occasion.

Providing the Fundamentals

Not too long ago, people called the physical education teacher the "gym teacher," and that teacher would teach "gym class." Can you imagine a big box with a high ceiling, a sweaty-smelling room, teaching students? Of course you can't. That's because a gym doesn't teach students—a physical education teacher who teaches in the gym teaches students. We also don't teach a big box with a high ceiling, a sweaty-smelling room, to students. We teach physical education to students, not the "gym." The skills these students learn in elementary school become the basis for the sports they play at higher levels and over their lifetime. Quality physical education teachers should take pride in this contribution. Here's a sampling of the approximate grades when skills for certain sports are taught. See how instrumental physical education teachers are in the development process.

Sport	Skills	Introduced
Football	Throwing	First grade
	Catching	First grade
	Kicking	First grade
	Punting	First grade
	Running	First grade
	Dodging	First grade
	Chasing	First grade
	Fleeing	First grade
	How to play	Fifth or sixth grade
	Team play	High school
Basketball	Throwing	First grade
	Catching	First grade
	Dribbling	First grade
	Running	First grade
	Dodging	First grade
	Chasing	First grade
	Fleeing	First grade
	How to play	Fifth or sixth grade
	Team play	High school
Gymnastics	Tumbling	First grade
Dance	Rhythmically moving	First grade
Baseball	Striking	First grade
	How to play	Fifth or sixth grade
	Team play	High school

Prehistoric Physical Education

The theory behind physical education has always made sense: everyone needs a sound body, not just a sound mind. We all function better if our bodies are in good shape. Exercise stimulates our thinking and creates a feeling of well-being. According to an article in the February 1996 issue of *Newsweek*, "Physical activity is good not only for the heart, but also for the brain, feeding it glucose and oxygen, and increasing nerve connections, all of which makes it easier for children of all ages to learn. Numerous studies show that children who exercise do better in school." The following research links movement to learning:

- Eric Jensen performed studies linking movement to learning showing that motor skills are fundamental to learning.
- *The Brain Gym* is a journal from the Education Kinesiology Foundation. The EKF publishes this journal three times a year as well as other documentation on exercise and the brain as part of a mission to enhance living and learning through the science of movement.

The Greeks, creators of the original Olympics, and other Europeans laid the foundation for physical education in America. People in history helped to provide models for a physical education program: John Locke, who wrote a book about the importance of a sound mind in a sound body; Johann GutsMuths, considered the "grandfather of physical education"; and Dudley Sargent, one of the most influential physical education leaders in the United States. When Boston became the first city to require daily exercise for students in 1853, physical education was growing in importance and value. You can find out more about the foundations of physical education by reading such books as *Physical Education, A Contemporary Introduction* by Angela Lumpkin.

Physical education started with noble goals and great ideals. Then certain issues got in the way. Unqualified individuals received jobs as physical education teachers, without the proper training or desire to teach quality physical education. Low-paying teaching jobs forced some good teachers to choose other options as a career. Veteran teachers who lost the desire to keep up with technology, new methods, and innovations also lost students' interest in the physical education program. The lack of merit-pay potential for teachers brought about apathy among some teachers. A big problem became burnout. The teachers who fall under this category may still be around today. Luckily, fresh or renewed quality PE teachers are surfacing to replace or replenish the "prehistoric" teacher.

"And one, and two, and three," hollers the large, muscular physical education teacher as he strains to make the students perform the monotonous calisthenics. He fiercely blows the whistle, which is hanging around his thick neck on a thin lanyard. He blows it to get attention from the students. He yells because his method of teaching is to frighten the students into performing what he wants them to do.

This stereotype is on its way out, but clearly there are many variations when you ask your friends or colleagues what their physical education classes were like when they were in school. I remember Mr. Sockalsburg, a physical education teacher from my first grade. He scared me away from ever wanting to pick up a basketball for years. I don't remember having a regular physical

education program; however, I remember this large man with a whistle, who yelled in a voice that echoed and vibrated your insides, visiting us once to teach us basketball. I don't remember anything else but being petrified to dribble that ball on those outside basketball courts with an extremely intimidating adult.

Mrs. Hoffman, however, the first consistent physical education teacher I can recall, from fifth grade, had a soft, Southern voice and was athletic yet beautiful. She could throw, catch, and perform any physical skill yet not appear intimidating or masculine, and both the boys and girls loved her.

When the physical education teacher in eighth grade told us to wrestle each other, my viewpoint on physical education changed again. The teachers, at the time, seemed to affect how I viewed the importance of physical education. When the physical education teacher made everyone perform flips and jumps on the trampoline, it was upsetting for those who didn't have the needed spatial awareness concepts of their bodies once off the ground. A classmate broke her arm trying to follow the teacher's commands. Another physical education teacher forced everyone to do a vault off of the springboard and my best friend broke her leg and was unable to cheerlead that year. Although, as a child, I loved army dodgeball, I still didn't think we should have played it every day, for the whole semester.

Some people you ask about their physical education experiences still can remember "prehistoric" physical education: "We played kickball every day." "We played army dodgeball." Or, "We worked out, or else. . . ." Every day that I had physical education, the classroom teacher would carry out that one bouncy, red playground ball. So the 25 of us would go outside and begin to participate in the activity. Some students would touch the ball and some would not. If you were lucky, you knew how to kick the ball hard, and how to catch the ball and field. The poor students who weren't as coordinated stood in the field and got hollered at for 30 minutes. Even if they did finally get a turn to kick, a ball hog or bully would try to convince them to give up their turn so that they could steal the turn and score—for the team's sake, of course.

Dodgeball added more insult to the insulted. Not only were the uncoordinated students intimidated by physical education, but now they were going to get hit, and possibly injured, in physical education class. All this, with a paid teacher promoting this scary dodgeball activity. The weak were the first targeted. Once they were pegged by the ball, they would check to see if all their body parts were still intact and then go sit on the sidelines and hope that this game wouldn't be over too soon, because they didn't want to have to go back in the game. Do you think they enjoyed physical education? Hardly. They couldn't wait for physical education time to end. They did not look forward to the 30 minutes of inaction and exposing their awkwardness.

The nonathletic students got their egos further squelched when we had to pick teams. Everyone wanted to be captain. Everyone wanted to pick the best student first. Everyone picked first felt great! Everyone picked last was humiliated and discouraged. The students picked last counted the minutes before PE time was over.

No wonder physical education sometimes has a bad rap. This is why we are struggling today, as quality physical education teachers—we still have this stigma attached to us. One positive aspect of the "prehistoric" physical education program is that it provides us with the driving power to do what it takes to promote physical education in a positive fashion—each day that we are teaching quality.

Being in so many schools, in so many cities, states, and even countries, really allowed me to see all sides of physical education: the good, the bad, and the ugly. With my love for sports I continued with my desire to search for a career involving sports through college. I fell in love with the atmosphere of the physical education building at George Mason University in Fairfax, Virginia, and adopted physical education as a major. Everyone in that building seemed so upbeat and energetic. It just made me feel healthy being in the building.

Becoming a PE teacher was not my goal as a physical education major. Even though I enjoyed physical education class, I saw some programs I wouldn't want to be a part of. A portion of the physical education experience called for visiting a school for 40 hours, just to see if we might like to pursue the teaching-track part of physical education. I witnessed some negligent practices. I thought that I could do a much better job: "What if I did this?" "The kids would love to do this." "I wish I could do this for the students." And, "If he would change the activity to this, then the students wouldn't be so bored."

This desire to design and deliver quality physical education that every child deserves prompted me to make my plans to become a genuine physical education teacher.

Physical Education Today

Physical education today should be dynamic, fair, educational, and rewarding. If it's not, we aren't doing anyone any good. If a student can't testify that physical education is worthwhile, then why have it? The challenge today is to overcome any damage to the reputations of physical educators and go beyond "prehistoric" teaching habits.

The inappropriate and stale ways are easy to duplicate: just throw out the ball, yell a little bit so they know who's boss, and sit back. That's a lot easier than using a lot of equipment, encouraging others, demonstrating, correcting, planning, supervising, and teaching. Worse is when a vibrant new teacher gets a physical education placement in a school with an intimidating department head who knows that his way is "the right way." Down the tubes go all the excitement and ideas this new instructor can bring to the school, because the "new kid on the block" does not want to rock the boat. So poor instructors still are being produced because the stale ones remain in business. Remember, you've got to rock the boat sometimes.

Also troublesome are the colleges that offer physical education courses that still preach prehistorically. Until the ancient ways are mended, the new and improved physical education will continue to struggle to overcome. There are so many ways to have a great program—keep trying and do everything to make yours and other physical education programs excel. Attend seminars, subscribe to good magazines, share with colleagues, buy a new book each year about physical education to keep up with new and noteworthy information, attend workshops, invent new games, keep an open mind, ask students for their input, use the World Wide Web, and get involved with technology. If you are reading this book, you already are contributing to the quest for better physical education programs and are one more step in the right direction.

Beam Me Up, Coach

May the force of other quality physical education teachers be with you. What kind of physical preparation will we need a thousand years, a hundred years, or even 10 years from now? Will laptops be on our list for school supplies? Will athletic shoes be required for physical education or will it be moon boots?

Heart-rate monitors, computers, videotaping, and automatic gadgets are all part of the current trends in physical education. How much we use these to improve our programs is what makes the difference in what the future holds for us. If we don't attempt to grow and keep up with the new gadgets, we will be "stuck in the past," thinking that we know what works and what doesn't.

Keep up with what's current. Even if you don't like or agree with what's "all the rage," you always should be well informed! When athletic shoes came out, it was important to athletes to wear a shoe that improved their running. Where would we be without our athletic shoes? When the oversized graphite or fiberglass tennis racket came out, there was a lot of resistance. But now look, do you know anyone who plays tennis and still uses a small wooden racket? So if rocket boots become popular and people are blasting off in their shoes, take note, and be ready for what might develop.

If we keep the focus of providing a challenging, rewarding physical education program at the forefront of our minds as we teach, whatever the future flashes before us can be used to help physical education grow. Reputable guidelines such as Developmentally Appropriate Physical Education Practices for Children, by National Association for Sports and Physical Education (NASPE), are great resources for designing quality physical education programs. Even if we're training in space suits or playing laser tag with laser guns, as long as our philosophy remains strong and supportive of students performing to the best of their ability, physically, the "quality" physical education teacher will thrive.

Sensible Alternative in Teaching Physical Education

OK, so you know you don't want to teach the Stone Age physical education. You are aware of the problems of some current physical education programs. Who knows what's in store with the Star Wars physical education? What is the best way to teach PE?

Every teaching style and every teacher is unique. If you keep the following ideas, thoughts, and guidelines in your daily teaching, you will be successful in teaching quality physical education. These are sample guidelines—make sure yours are sound and beneficial to the students, first and foremost.

Philosophy of Physical Education

Here are some goals to keep in mind when teaching physical education classes:

- To provide positive experiences involving physical skills, lifetime sports activities, fitness activities, and health so that students may have the knowledge and skill base to live a healthy and fulfilling life.
- To create an environment in which each student can successfully explore the principles of health, fitness, and sport.
- To offer students opportunities to develop physical skills, health awareness, and fitness and to participate in sports and recreational activities.
- To emphasize that without your health, you can't function optimally mentally, so training in physical fitness and health is vital.

Curriculum

Consider the following:

- How many days will you have physical education per week?
- What will you teach?
- What are your state's standards?
- Do you test students in fitness testing?

Think about what your goals are for your program:

- To provide a well-rounded physical movement class for a certain amount of days per week.
- To provide opportunities to excel in improving fitness level.
- To meet the state standards as well as other important issues.
- To link physical education to other areas of life.

Yearly Plan

An example of a yearly plan is to cover some principles of fitness. Provide experiences in the following:

- Throwing
- Catching
- Fitness
- Dance

- Kicking
- Dribbling
- Movement education
- Striking
- Volleying
- Gymnastics
- Games

Also, cover some health issues:

- Muscles
- Bones
- First aid
- Hygiene
- Safety

Unit Plan

Following is a sample monthly unit plan for once-a-week physical education. All days must include some time for fitness, sometimes a test or practice fitness test, and all days must include some health education.

August

First week—movement education

September

First week—throwing introduction
Second week—throwing revisit
Third week—throwing refining
Fourth week—throwing in games

October

First week—catching introduction
Second week—catching revisit
Third week—catching refining
Fourth week—catching in games

November

First week—movement education

Second week—volleying introduction

Third week—volleying revisit

Fourth week—volleying refining/games

December

First week—dribbling with hands introduction

Second week—dribbling with hands revisit

Third week—dribbling with feet introduction

Fourth week—dribbling with feet revisit

January

First week—dribbling with an implement introduction

Second week—gymnastics introduction

Third week—gymnastics revisit

Fourth week—gymnastics refining

February

First week—dance introduction

Second week—dance revisit

Third week—dance refining

Fourth week—kicking introduction

March

First week—kicking revisit

Second week—kicking refining

Third week—kicking games

Fourth week—striking introduction

April

First week—striking revisit

Second week—striking refining

Third week—striking games

Fourth week—Spring Break

May

First week—movement education

Second week—fitness testing wrap-up

Third week—special-events sports, games

Fourth week—special-events sports, games

Insert Field Day into the schedule

Following is a sample monthly unit plan for five-day-a-week physical education. Introduce a skill on Mondays, and assess students on Fridays. Each week have a health topic.

August

Movement activities

September

First week—fitness activities

Second week—throwing

Third week—catching

Fourth week—kicking

October

First week—fitness activities/movement activities

Second week—volleying

Third week—dribbling with hands

Fourth week—striking

November

First week—fitness activities/movement activities

Second week—special physical education activity games

Third week—dance

Fourth week—dribbling with feet

December

First week—fitness activities/movement activities

Second week—throwing

Third week—catching

Fourth week—special activities

January

First week—fitness activities/movement activities

Second week—gymnastics

Third week—gymnastics

Fourth week—dance

February

First week—fitness activities/movement activities

Second week—special physical activity games

Third week—dribbling with hands

Fourth week—striking

March

First week—fitness activities/movement activities

Second week—volleying

Third week—kicking

Fourth week—dribbling with implements

April

First week—fitness activities/movement activities

Second week—games

Third week—special activities

Fourth week—Spring Break

May

First week—fitness testing wrap-up

Second week—final skills wrap-up (one skill each day for the next two weeks)

Third week—same as second week

Fourth week—Field Day prep, Field Day, and Special Event Week

If you follow the guidelines and ideas provided by this book, you should have a successful quality PE program. The world needs good, strong programs provided by hardworking teachers. You can be one of them!

Crack the Codes

Even the best job in the world takes knowing the ins and outs and tricks of the trade. Here's your helpful guide to facing and overcoming the many adventures and misadventures that you are about to encounter.

Your mission always will be tougher than you had planned! Expect that, and accept that. This is part of what makes teaching exciting, challenging, and rewarding. So every day that you look at your plan book, keep in mind the word "tentative." That's important for physical education teachers. Insert that word in your plan book to relieve some pressure, tension, and aggravation.

What if your plan is foiled? You are unable to use the field, the gym, the cafeteria, or the classroom. The mission is not impossible—don't despair. Turn to the page in this book that covers the problem you are having, and we'll remedy this concern. Turn on the "Mission Impossible" track on your compact disc now and let's crack the codes.

Whatever the problem or concern is, consider that to be your obstacle. That will be the title you look for when you need help. Here is what to look for in the pages that follow in order to crack the codes and get the most out of this book:

Obstacle: the situation that is causing you to have to think more than you want to

Common Mistakes: what many physical education teachers might do without thoroughly thinking through the problem

Solutions: the ways to hurdle over the obstacle with the least amount of pain and agony

Tips:

Ideas to help you

Ways to decrease the size of the obstacle

Ways to get around the obstacle without tackling it head on

A method for avoiding the obstacle entirely

Real-Life Story: a real-life tale of events that have occurred

These "codes" and the information that follows will assist you and prepare you for the concerns that plague every quality physical education teacher. Remember, though, that every situation is going to be unique, because every human is unique. Good luck on your mission!

chapter 1

BE CLOTHES-MINDED

FLIP-FLOP 50-YARD DASH

Pumping, digging, and running his heart out, Seth started his 50-yard sprint to the finish. While he was pushing past Jerome and Michael, he looked intense and strong. Then his stride started to break up a little bit, and Jerome and Michael passed him. When Seth was flying into the fast lane, a flimsy white flip-flop flew off his foot. Seth had ran out of his shoes.

His shoe choice of the day was a 99-cent pair of flip-flops. It was warm outside and maybe he wanted to be at the beach. Or maybe these are the cool things to wear, like Birkenstocks or Flojos were in their time. Actually, Seth was wearing them because he didn't have any other shoes that fit.

Obstacle

> Making sure that students are wearing the proper shoes to ensure their safety.

Common Mistakes

- Permitting students to participate with unsafe shoes.
- Not asking students why they didn't wear the proper shoes.

Solutions

- Do a brief shoe check. You can even announce it, if you want to make it known to everyone. That way, the students know that you are doing it and that they will have to be accountable for their shoes.

- Do not allow students to participate with open-toed or heeled shoes. Show them what an athletic shoe looks like. Explain that this is the best shoe for PE because it enables them to run and change direction and it will protect their feet. It also will not fall off when they run, as long as they lace it properly.

- If a student cannot afford shoes, or has missed physical education more than three times because of shoes, ask the nurse if she could provide assistance. The nurse could be the third party to offer shoes and to call the parent. This way the parents don't have to be embarrassed talking to the teacher. And the best thing is, the student gets the help and assistance that he needs.

Tip

If a student likes to participate and is not permitted because of his shoes, he will hate sitting out so much that he will not forget again to wear the proper physical education shoes.

Real-Life Story

Seth's mother couldn't afford to buy shoes, so he always wore flip-flops. The physical education teacher asked his regular classroom teacher to offer Seth a pair of shoes that an anonymous person had left. Seth took them home to ask his mother. He then wore the shoes, and he participated for the rest of the year.

"YOUR BUTT'S FALLING OUT"

On your mark, get set, go!

Off they go, running as fast as their legs will carry them. They are neck and neck as they near the halfway mark of the race. Suddenly a fellow student watching from the sidelines shouts, "Hey, your butt's falling out!"

Instant laughter and finger pointing erupt from the sidelined students as they stare at Jerome's white underwear. Jerome is "stylin'," and he likes to look cool while sporting jeans that hang halfway off his rear end. He has to make a split-second decision: "Do I stop and fix my pants? Or do I keep running and risk further embarrassment?"

As a responsible teacher, you have to offer some kind of response here, too!

Obstacle

Getting students to dress appropriately for physical activity.

Common Mistakes

- Ignoring the situation.
- Overreacting to the situation.

Solutions

- Explain lightheartedly that if Jerome were in the Olympics years ago he would have fit in, because athletes ran in the nude. However, in the 21st century, students must be clothed and have their private areas fully covered with school-acceptable clothing.
- Insist that the student wouldn't let anything stop him from winning or finishing a race if he were in the Olympics! So tell him to grab those pants and yank them in one hand and run his hardest. That's the risk one takes when choosing fashion over sense.
- Require uniforms for physical education.
- Set appropriate, reasonable guidelines that are approved by your principal for participating in physical education. Hand these out at the beginning of the school year.

Tips

- Explain to the students about Speedos. These aren't for the men and boys to show off their masculinity; they're to keep everything tightly tucked in. If someone dove into a pool with loose-fitting shorts, he would be mooning everyone.

- Explain about men's wrestling outfits, running shorts, and football tights in the same manner as you'd explain Speedos.
- Discuss the late Olympic runner Florence Griffith Joyner ("Flo Jo"). She ran with great fashion and style, was beautiful, and her clothes never hindered her performance.
- Keep flag-football belts, or cotton ropes, handy for "saggers."

Real-Life Story

Jerome's story is from real life. As a result of his incident, he now asks ahead of time if we are going to test for the mile or race. He also is not too proud to ask for a belt.

In another real-life example, during a jumping-rope activity, Cory began to jump. He was on the verge of being really "cool." As he confidently brought the rope around his body for a jump, on the flight upward, his fashionable baggy Levi's slipped all the way past his waist, over his hips, not even hitting the thighs, in one single motion, to his ankles. His hands were above his head with the rope still grasped. He gave the fifth-grade girls quite a giggle. Cory was cool, and he pulled them up fast and attempted to blow it off by doing a few more jumps. Cory might have been a "cool dude," but his face was on fire with embarrassment that day.

DRESSES AND MONKEY BARS

Peanut butter and jelly, ham and cheese, Tom and Jerry, pizza and beer—all naturally fit together. However, some combinations are so obviously unnatural they are a natural disaster. Dresses and monkey bars are an example of a big no-no, a no-way fit!

You'd think that some things would go without saying, right? But, as soon as you don't say it, it happens. The clash of the dresses and monkey bars occurs right there in your class, in front of not only your eyes but all the boys' eyes, too! Now the boys can't stop pointing and laughing. What in the world was this girl thinking, and will she be able to face all the boys now that she flashed her "frillies" in their faces?

Obstacle

> Preventing the embarrassing monkey bars show and other indecent acts.

Common Mistakes

- Pretending that it didn't happen.
- Ignoring the situation—parents will call you if they think there is anything unusual or suspicious going on.

Solutions

- Set down rules for dressing appropriately in physical education class:

   > All girls who wear dresses or skirts to class must wear shorts underneath.

   > Shirts and shorts should not expose any private part of the body (i.e., any part that has an "embarrassing" name).

- Set down rules for activities:

   > To do tumbling skills, students must have shorts on if they are wearing a dress or skirt.

   > When they climb anything, those with dresses or skirts must have on shorts underneath.

- Stress that the reason for this is to stay on task and to save anybody from embarrassment.

Tip

> Use the following "Real-Life Story" as an example to your classes so that the girls always can remember the "girl in the dress on the monkey bars."

Real-Life Story

Peggy was always "prissy." She wore dresses a lot. She also liked to play on the playground. One day Peggy flashed her panties to everyone in the third grade, while she gracefully grabbed one bar and then reached for the other on the monkey bars. She screamed once she realized that the boys were all pointing at her frilly underpants. From that day on, for years and years, she was known as "Pretty Panties Peggy."

SPICE GIRL SHOES

"Let's start off with a quarter-mile warm-up today," shouts the physical education teacher with great enthusiasm. "Yeah!" yell the students as they scramble past one another as if they are in a race.

Sometimes you start the activity instantly so that the students are doing something immediately. There isn't time to check thoroughly for proper clothing.

Speedy Susan is way behind everyone today, so you wondered what could be wrong with her. She finally struts in and you see the culprit: those quirky, 3-inch platform shoes worn by the singing group the Spice Girls. Whether the Spice Girls are all the rage or another trendy teenage phenomenon has captured students' attention, there always will be some fad that will entice students to wear what they see others wearing.

Even though Susan is fast, sports and athletics have lost to fashion in this round! Spice Girls 1, physical education 0, in today's meet.

Obstacle

Getting students to wear the proper shoes for physical education.

Common Mistake

Not paying attention to what shoes students are wearing.

Solutions

- Just like the flip-flops, Spice Girl shoes are unsafe. The student will have to sit out of physical education for a day.

- Give the student a friendly reminder note to take home:

> Dear Susan,
> Please be safe in PE! Remember the proper shoes for class.
> —*The Physical Education Department*

(Place a picture of a shoe on the letter.)

- If someone does this consistently, on purpose to get out of class, speak to her. Let her know the dangers and that you're on to her. Calling home should remedy the situation. Ask the parents if the child still can run with the shoes, with their permission, if she forgets. If they say yes, then have the student take the lap and participate. If they say no, then hopefully they will help the student remember to bring athletic shoes to class.

- Suggest putting athletic shoes in a backpack so that they are always there.

Tip

If a student doesn't come with athletic shoes, and the phone call home doesn't work, see if the family can afford athletic shoes by asking the classroom teacher or principal. If the family can't afford athletic shoes, ask for donations of athletic shoes from other adults that have kids.

Real-Life Story

Morningview Elementary held its spur-of-the-moment Spring Speed Sprint Challenge on the day that Sarah came to school wearing Spice Girl shoes. Sarah could outrun everyone in fourth grade. She loved to compete and run. Unfortunately, she was not permitted to participate because her shoes were unsafe. She cried and pouted. Now, Sarah carries a change of shoes with her to school so that she can be stylish in the classroom and in physical education.

THE UNIFORM ISSUE

Jerome's rear end is hanging out. Susan's Spice Girl shoes are "stylin'" but are unacceptable. Seth is trying to fly in the 50 wearing his flip-flops. Peggy is wearing the cutest little dress, but with no shorts. If Betsy bends over in that shirt, her chest will pop out. Fashion, maybe; sensible and safe, maybe not.

At another school, the students are all wearing the same thing: Shorts that are the appropriate length, with an elastic waistband. No more rear ends falling out. T-shirts with crew necks. No more breast bulge. But there is still the concern with the shoes. Is this uniform necessary? Do the students like it? Is it safer?

Obstacle

Figuring out whether your students should wear a PE uniform.

Common Mistakes

- Thinking it will solve all your clothing issues.
- Having to still worry about:

  shoes;

  the cost of uniforms (it's minimal, but what if the parent is on free breakfast and lunch and can't even dress the child now?);

  uniform checks;

  whether to take points off for no uniform;

  a time factor for changing clothes; and

  locker-room issues.

Solution

If your school supports it, and can afford it, physical education uniforms could be a great idea. Additionally, ask if the classroom teachers could supervise the students while they change clothes. This will really help, plus allow you to save your physical education action time. It takes students a long time to change clothes. Do you want to waste minutes on dressing out? What if you only have them once a week, for 30 minutes? If it takes them five minutes to dress and five minutes to change back—which is excellent timing for a whole class—you've cut your physical education time to 20 minutes.

Tips

- Uniforms can be purchased for a very minimal charge. Unless you are in a severely poor school area, they are affordable.
- Kids don't have to worry about ruining their school clothes in physical education class when they have uniforms.

Real-Life Story

After all the effort and thought to wear uniforms, Susan changes into her physical education uniform and tops it off with a little bit of spice. She has on 3-inch platform Sporty Spice Girl shoes. You win some, you lose some.

2

KIDS SAY THE DARNEDEST THINGS

"I CAN'T—I THINK I HAVE ADHD"

Catching asthma is as easy to catch as attention deficit hyperactivity disorder (ADHD). Be careful—if you are too close to someone, you could catch it!

Students will have some wild excuses. Ashley told her physical education teacher that she couldn't run because she thought she had ADHD. Students hear the other students' excuses flying around, and when they think they've got a handle on them, they test one out to see if it will fly.

For those genuine ADHD students, physical education is the best thing for them. For those looking for an excuse, the physical education teacher has a job to do.

Obstacle

> Sorting out the real ADHD students from the wanna-be sick students, and giving both the proper treatment.

Common Mistake

> Letting students get away with things because they say they have an illness.

Solutions

ADHD is not contagious. Students who have it get a lot of attention from their classroom teachers to get on task. This attention is mostly negative, but it is attention. The students who want attention might envy the students with ADHD because of the attention they get. Keep the ADHD students on task by involving them and using proximity and reinforcement often.

Students with ADHD do not want to sit out, so if they are off task, do the following:

- Remind them to get on task.
- If they continue to be disruptive, sit them out. They will ask to get back in as soon as possible.
- Bring the student back in as soon as he realizes what he has done and can correct it.
- Remember that they want to fidget, move, scream, holler, run, wiggle, stretch, jump, spin, talk, and not be still. They don't want to sit out and watch, so there is your biggest solution—getting the child to be responsible for his behavior so that he won't have

to sit out. Physical education is great for this real ADHD person. The ADHD child should be successful in physical education because in our class you "do" things!

Tip

You only have these students for about 45 minutes. So, do your best to keep the ADHD students on task while they participate in an activity that is great for their bodies and minds.

Real-Life Story

David was always so excited and fidgety. He drove his classroom teacher crazy. But, when he was in physical education, he knew that he had to control himself or he wouldn't have the chance to participate. He would get off task, and then realize it, or the teacher would remind him, and then he would snap right back into good behavior. He often would be a model student.

"I CAUGHT AN ASTHMA"

I hear the second-graders running by and then I hear a "plunk." As the students begin their quarter-mile jog around the grassy track, 20 energetic runners speed pass me. One slightly plump boy hesitates and plunks himself, lifelessly, down to the ground.

"Carl, what's wrong? Why aren't you running today?" I ask. "Oh, well, you see, over the weekend we had some company, and I must have caught an asthma from them. So I can't run anymore," is Carl's matter-of-fact reply.

As quality physical education teachers, we know about asthma. You've heard the saying "what they don't know won't hurt them." But it's what the students think they know that does the real hurting.

Obstacles

- Weak excuses to get out of physical activities.
- Students' perceptions of medical conditions (e.g., Carl's perception: "If Joey gets out of running because of this 'asthma' thing, then I can say that I caught it, too. Then I won't have to run.")
- Your lack of knowledge of medical conditions.

Common Mistakes

- Allowing the student to get away with such excuses.
- Not knowing about the condition the student is complaining about.

Solutions

- Know about the condition: asthma is a chronic disorder characterized by panting, wheezing, coughing, and difficulty in breathing. It is not contagious through "visiting company" or by physical contact.
- As for other conditions, review the students' medical information! That's a must. Your school nurse should have a list of students with medical concerns.

Tips

- Ask for a doctor's note. Let students know that they must participate unless they have a note from a doctor, nurse, or parent.

- Use this moment as a teachable moment for the students. Briefly, discuss the medical condition with the students, as a group, so that they know and understand what asthma is.
- Tell them a true victory story: For example, Jackie Joyner-Kersee, who has asthma, is one of the fastest runners in the world!

Real-Life Story

Carl was told immediately that one can't catch asthma as he had suggested. The above victory story was described to him, and without any further talking, off he zoomed around the track.

"MY MAMA SAYS SWEATING GIVES YOU BUMPS"

"Phew!" the first-grader said to his physical education teacher. "Doesn't sweating make you hungry? It makes me hungry because people smell like cooked potatoes when they sweat!" This innocent statement was made after the child had run for 30 minutes in 90-degree heat, with beads of sweat dripping down his face.

Some kids love to play in the heat and sun. What about the others? They may have gotten used to that pumping air conditioning as they play their video games. When they actually go out to *do* something, they can't take the "realness" of it, that is, actually participating in something instead of watching it.

Worse is when their parents tell the children things that reinforce their behavior. One fifth-grader, who was a good runner throughout the year, transformed into a slacker in the hot weather. When he was approached and asked what was going on, he surprised everyone when he said, "My mama says sweating gives you bumps." He was a good athlete with potential, which was about to fall prey to an old wives' tale and the adolescent worry about how he looks. He had seen people with pimples and acne, and he valued his looks too much to ruin them by running, he thought. And all it took was for his mother to tell him something like "sweating gives you pimples."

Obstacle

> How do you convince adolescents that sweating and being physical is cool and healthy, not detrimental?

Common Mistakes

- Not fighting this behavior.
- Letting them get away with this thinking and become lazy.

Solutions

- Here's your selling point. This is your chance to dispel the myths: Tell the students that it's when the body is not healthy that the skin starts to react poorly. A cause of acne is hormones. At this point in the adolescent's life, the hormones are causing the irritation of the skin. Stress also can help cause acne.
- It is a well-known fact that exercise helps to reduce stress. So, if a person reduces the stress, she reduces the chance of getting bumps.
- Let students know that fresh air and sunlight are good for the skin. Too much sun, however—like a sunburn—is not.

Tips

- Get pictures of athletes who are examples of acne-free faces.
- Tell the students that if they have bumps or acne, they can check out solutions, with their parents, using over-the-counter remedies. If that doesn't work, they can see their doctor or a dermatologist.

Real-Life Story

To be good-looking, Rakeem thought that he shouldn't have acne, shouldn't smell, shouldn't get his cool shoes dirty, and should do whatever it took to look good. Rakeem demanded a lot of the physical education teacher's time, so she invested it in confidence building and reinforcing the positive need for health and fitness to improve, not sacrifice, the person's appearance. Rakeem was a leader in his grade level, so this time was well invested! Rakeem took his chances by trusting his physical education teacher, and he found out for himself that she was right. When Rakeem does something, his classmates watch and take note. So the time invested also helped all the other students in Rakeem's class.

"I BEAT"

"I beat," boasted the proud third-grader. Well, what did he beat? Did he beat the drums? Did he beat up the batter for a cake? Did he beat somebody up? This is an English lesson in need.

The boy had just finished racing someone, and he had won. Instead of humbly carrying on with the next task, he boasted to everyone, "I beat." It reminds me of an ape or caveman who only knows a few words and can't conjugate verbs or speak well. "I beat, I beat, I beat."

People have a natural desire to want to do things well. If you do something very well, you can be rewarded with monetary awards, trophies, medals, ribbons, and recognition. It's great to be first. It's great when you win a race or a team game or competition. It feels so good—you're on top of the world.

If you are already on top of the world, why boast about it? This is what we, as quality PE teachers, must enforce. Good sporting behavior involves winning and losing gracefully.

Some educators think that competition should be eliminated altogether. The idea of throwing out all competition is sad—for me, for the students, and for the whole world. The world, naturally, has competition in it, so to ignore that fact would be ignorant.

If you teach good sporting behavior, and a little English, then you and your students can enjoy the feeling of being first, or winning—not beating.

Obstacle

Helping students understand how to win and lose gracefully.

Common Mistakes

- Avoiding all competition.
- Allowing the winners to be boastful.

Solutions

- Teach good sporting behavior—every day!
- Give positive feedback, enormously, to the person who genuinely displays good sporting behavior.
- Make this so important that it becomes natural.
- Make it so natural that the winner would never think about boasting and making another person feel bad.
- Be consistent about good sporting behavior, with both winners and losers.

- State that, in the English language, the proper way of exclaiming victory is saying "I won" and not "I beat." The latter means either that you hit someone or that you didn't finish your sentence.

Tips

- Give a weekly good-sporting-behavior certificate.
- Have competitions that not only allow the good athletes to win, but others as well:

  Improving one's own score

  Doing silly races (e.g., a sack race, a three-legged race)

  Answering questions
- Make the competition accessible and, of course, lots of fun!

Real-Life Story

Don sat down and started to cry one day. When the teacher asked him why, he said, "I'm the slowest boy in the class." The teacher couldn't dispute that, but she said, "For goodness sake, Don, the only time you need to have speed in real life is if you are running out of the way of a car or running away from a bear in the forest, which you probably won't have to do. Otherwise, don't worry about how fast you are compared to your classmates. Any other time you play a sport you won't worry about who finishes last, but about enjoying the game." Don looked up, smiled, and said, "You're right."

"IT HURTS WHEN I DO THIS"

As the students walk by the physical education teacher, they take every opportunity to get her to focus on them. "Look, I did this while skateboarding," says a third-grader, showing her his bandage as he walks from the gym to the activity area. Johnny points to a cut on his arm as he passes by the teacher. Kathy comes up holding her finger, tightly, and says, "It hurts when I do this," as she squeezes her jammed finger.

As the teacher, your first instinct is to say, "Well, don't do that." What these students are really doing is looking for you to notice and pay attention to them. They like your attention.

Obstacle

How do you handle the complaints of aches and pains?

Common Mistakes

- Blowing the students off.
- Making students feel unimportant.

Solutions

- Give eye contact to each student as he walks by you in line.
- Give students the attention that they seek and listen to them briefly. Then encourage them to be safe and to try to work through the injury by doing the lesson to the best of their ability.
- Make sure you tell them at the beginning of the year to get notes if they have a serious injury or illness. Tell them to see you in the morning before class if they have a note. So, when class begins, you don't have any wasted time.
- You should know that if you look at an injury, it makes it feel better. Live by this one!

Tip

The saying, "It hurts when I do this," still can be remedied with, "Well, don't do that," but add, "Try doing this."

Real-Life Story 📖

Sally came up to show the physical education teacher a cut. She said that she had just got cut by someone. Sally just wanted a little attention—the cut was barely there and was at least three days old. So the teacher said, "I see your cut. Wow, it didn't happen today, but how did you do it?" This did the following:

- It got the teacher's attention.
- It made Sally aware that the teacher can't be fooled but can be concerned.
- It gave Sally a chance to tell her story truthfully.

A few seconds later, her frown turned into a smile, and the teacher had her scooting on her way back on task.

"I GOTTA CRAP"

Sometimes students say things that are funny. Sometimes they say things that are distasteful. This student said a little bit of both. He ran up to the teacher and said, "I gotta crap." He was sweaty and making a distorted face. His forearm and hand were wrapped across his stomach as he leaned over. The teacher thought that he needed to use the restroom, bad!

Surely, children know that the word "crap" is not an appropriate word to use in front of a teacher! The teacher couldn't believe that the student had said that. So, she bent down and said, "You need to use a different word than the one you just used, especially when speaking to a teacher."

The student looked at the teacher in pain and said, "Well, what are you supposed to call it?" The teacher asked, "What did your parents teach you to say?" He replied, "I don't get any craps at home." The teacher thought that was peculiar and asked a few more questions.

It turns out that the student didn't have to go to the restroom at all. Because of the way some students speak, and hear other students speak, certain words are not pronounced properly. Either from ignorance or innocence, they will mispronounce words. The student really had a cramp, from running.

Obstacles

- Weeding through the lazy talk, the slang, and the words that students think they are saying correctly and in the right context.
- Trying not to offend students when they speak.

Common Mistakes

- Hurting a student's feelings.
- Not correcting the improper pronunciation and the improper choice of words.

Solutions

- Say "Excuse me?" to the student and let him repeat what he just said. If he repeats it, see if he knows what it means. If he thinks it is correct, in a positive way, tell him the correct way to say the word in the right context.

- If the student repeats it, and knows what it means, don't permit him to use poor language in your class. Tell him how offensive and embarrassing it is for him when he speaks ignorantly. Let him know that it makes him look like he isn't very smart.

- If the student doesn't repeat what he has said, then he knows it was inappropriate. Show your disappointment and disapproval and explain that a student should always show respect for a teacher and for himself. After all, a teacher wouldn't say rude things in front of her students.

Tip

Use yourself as an example and discuss how you speak to others. If you spoke ignorantly, people wouldn't respect you or understand you.

Real-Life Story

When this student used the improper term, he realized he showed his ignorance, and he was embarrassed enough to be conscious of what he had said, even if it was only around the teacher. That is an important start.

"GRAB YOUR BALLS"

"Grab your balls and begin," says the physical education teacher to the class of fifth-graders. Instantly, a whirlwind of laughter blows over her students. Then they start saying, "Ooh, gross," or, "I'm not going to do that." If you've got some real smart-aleck students in your class, then you may see a few grab their crotch. Hopefully, they are more respectful than that. If you say that phrase, it's hard to escape without a snicker or a turning of the heads to look at each other's reaction.

Obstacles

- Saying the "balls" phrase—it's going to come up over and over.
- Watching what you say, so that it cannot be turned into a comical, sexual situation.

Common Mistakes

- Not thinking through your phrases before you say them.
- Running words together, or getting lazy with words.

Solutions

- Be clear when you are speaking.
- Instead of, "Grab your balls," say, "Grab your basketballs."
- Instead of, "Hand your balls to …," say, "Hand your volleyballs to …"
- Instead of, "Let's start with the breast," say, "Let's start our swim with the breaststroke."
- Instead of, "Spread your legs," say, "Separate your legs so that they are apart."

Tips

- It's better to be clear than to risk the embarrassment.
- One slip of the tongue could throw off your whole class. Depending on the age and type of students at your school, this could mean the difference between a giggle and a giant outburst.

Real-Life Story

It only took one slip for a first-year teacher to stop and think before he ever said the blanket statement of "grab your balls" again. The rudeness and boldness of some of the male students and the awkwardness of the female students to their reactions made it necessary to speak very clearly from that point on.

"ROLL 'EM"

"Lights, camera . . . roll 'em."

"Rollin', rollin', rollin' on the river, la, la, la."

"Roll with it."

"I'm going to roll up my hair to get some curls."

"Let's rock 'n' roll."

"Roll 'em up, dude."

"Stop, drop, and roll."

"We're having rolls with dinner tonight."

"Roll it nice and smooth down the alley."

If you were a first- or second-grader and you heard the word "roll," you might have one of these thoughts rolling through your mind—hopefully not the risqué ones, though. So, how do the students know which "roll" definition to choose?

Remember Amelia Bedelia? When she was told to "draw" the drapes or blinds, she took a pencil and sketch pad and drew them on paper, instead of going to the window. She knew a definition for a word, but she didn't know the correct one to use.

The same thing will occur with students in physical education class. If you say a word with multiple meanings, be ready for some Amelia Bedelia action.

Obstacle

Saying words that have meanings other than the one you are intending to use.

Common Mistakes

- Assuming that the students understand what you mean when you use similar-sounding words with alternate meanings unintentionally (homonyms).
- Not being clear.

Solutions

- When you are discussing the "roll" that the students will be doing in class tomorrow, distinguish how they will do that skill.
- Especially explain when you are in an environment that would confuse the students.

If you are in the field and talking about "rolling," be sure they understand that it's not rolling in the grass and getting itchy and dirty. Although a lot of kids would love that! Some kids are allergic to grass. Explain that it is rolling a ball that they will do tomorrow.

When you are talking about "dribbling," many students only know about one kind of dribbling. So when you see a student using his finger pads while striking the ball downward with his hand, with a black-and-white soccer ball, don't be astonished. That's all that he knows.

Tips 🏃

- Have fun with homonyms! Play around with them. The kids will make you laugh with their innocence and naivete.

- Create lessons using homonyms. Ask the students to think about the following phrases and act upon them:

  "Trap the ball."

  "Slip on your coat."

  "Check your opponent."

  "Attack."

- Interlink your lessons with Standards of Learning and language arts.

- For the first- and second-graders, create an Amelia Bedelia lesson. Amelia Bedelia goes to physical education. . . .

Amelia Bedelia's teacher told her to *slip* on her PE tennis shoes. So, as if they were banana peels, she slipped and fell over her shoes. Amelia was ready for class, and she was *paying* attention to the physical education teacher. She only had nickels and dimes, though. The teacher told Amelia to *check* the line to see if everyone was ready. So, Amelia put a check next to the person on the line. The teacher told Amelia to *pick up* the pace of the line. So she tried to lift everyone up but she wasn't strong enough. Then the teacher told Amelia to *jump rope*, so Amelia jumped over and over the rope while it was on the ground. And then the teacher said *"take a lap,"* so Amelia plopped down into someone's lap while he was sitting. The teacher said that it was time to *roll*, so Amelia tucked her chin to her chest and did the prettiest forward rolls. The teacher said, "No, Amelia, that means our time is *up*." So Amelia looked up into the sky to see what time it was. "No, Amelia, it's time to *go*," said her teacher, so Amelia Bedelia ran to the bathroom to go, and off she went, to return again the next PE day.

Real-Life Story

The first-graders were in their huddle and the teacher told them to look forward to tomorrow because they were going to do lots of rolling in physical education. One student, who reacts adversely to grass, went home and told his father, with much displeasure, that they were going to roll all over the grass tomorrow. The father called the school and asked to speak to the physical education teacher who was going to force his child to roll in grass. When the teacher answered and said, "Sure, you bet we're going to roll in the grass," the father gasped. The teacher added, "And we will be throwing the balls and catching them as soon as we cover rolling-the-ball skills." The father simply said, "Oh, OK." Without any further explanation or embarrassment, they both said, "Have a great day," and hung up.

"HE SAID THE 'C' WORD"

Five frantic second-graders race up and all scream at you at once. They are all speaking at the same time, so you have no idea what is wrong. The commotion seems to be centered around a little boy named Jimmy. You wonder what in the world could be so important that all these students stop what they are doing to come to you and tattle. Finally, you convince them to speak one at a time. It turns out that our Jimmy has said a bad word. It was the "C" word, the students tell you. You're wondering, what's the "C" word? So you ask, "What word did he say?"

"He said 'can't,'" the students say with disgust, adding, "He just stopped trying." Then you remember stressing that they shouldn't say "can't," and that it was considered a bad word. You were trying to encourage students to be positive, and eliminate "can't" from their vocabulary, when tasks seemed too tough.

Obstacle

Beware of what you say because you have a captive audience. Remember that what you say is golden to these young, admiring students.

Common Mistakes

- Not watching what you say.
- Not taking advantage of a teaching opportunity while you have a captive audience.

Solutions

- Take advantage of your position to have students want to hang on your every word.
- Use this advantage to go above and beyond the physical skill that you are working on. Talk about something important in life skills or a current issue that's hot.

Tips

- Your influence on these students shouldn't go to waste. Get on your soapbox and help the students be the best they can be.
- Not saying "can't" is a great way for students not to give up on themselves. Hopefully, this will carry over into everything they do at school and at home!

Real-Life Story

The students knew that "can't" was not in our vocabulary during physical education class. Everyone was to try their hardest, and then try again, and then see if they could improve from when they first attempted the skill. After they looked at it in that perspective, the "I can't" turned into "I'll try."

HITTING, SHOOTING, STRIKING, JABBING, AND KICKING

"Mom, my teacher told me that we will be hitting, shooting, stabbing, jabbing, striking, and kicking people tomorrow in PE," said a first-grader when she got home from school one day. "What in the world is this crazy class? I don't want to get hurt in school. I don't want to go to school tomorrow!" she cried to her mother.

What is cool about physical education also can scare some students who don't know all the special PE phrases and action words: "Go for the kill." "Jab it." "It's dead." "Come on, just shoot." "Steal it." "Hit and run."

Obstacle

Getting kids excited in a scared sense, instead of a motivated sense.

Common Mistakes

- Not being clear to the younger, naive, innocent, and nonathletic students.
- Assuming that students will understand your terms.
- Using too much "shock" to motivate students.

Solutions

- Stay excited, but explain what there is to be excited about.
- Realize the maturity of the students you are speaking to before you shock or scare them from class.

Tips

Excite and then explain right away:

- "I can't wait until our next class! We will be kicking, shooting, tackling, and trapping. We won't be kicking, shooting, tackling, and trapping each other—we will do all of these actions with a ball. These are some of the things you can do in soccer."
- "John is going to be sneaky, go for the steal, and then shoot in our next class. We will be starting our March Madness. Be ready to throw, dribble, and catch a basketball."

Real-Life Story

Jeremy was so scared to go to school that his father came with him to check out what was going on in physical education. He realized what he was scared of, laughed, and had a discussion of "scary" PE terms with his son, on the spot. He laughed again, and then he left.

chapter

3

KIDS *DO* THE DARNEDEST THINGS

THE 40-MINUTE MILE

Fitness testing is welcomed by some, and also disliked by some. Mr. Hunt loved testing the mile run. He would get the students ready by having pacing, stride, breathing, and mental toughness lessons before the mile run/jog/walk test.

No matter how someone is doing, you must encourage her to try to do her best. Four fifth-grade girls passed Mr. Hunt on their quarter-mile first lap in four minutes. He didn't give up. "Good job, girls. Go a little faster and you can still make the national score," he shouted. "It's 12 minutes. Anyone can do a 12-minute mile. You could even walk some and still make it."

"Oh, did he say we could walk and make it?" asked one fifth-grader. "Yeah, we can walk and still make it," replied her friend.

People always hear what they want to hear, right? So Mr. Hunt continued to encourage his slowpokes. He told them that they had to jog as well, not solely walk. They sped by him with a second lap time of 10 minutes. After they realized they couldn't reach the national score, they stopped trying to jog. They passed Mr. Hunt with a time of 16 minutes on their third lap. Their fourth lap was a nice leisurely stroll around the track. Mr. Hunt congratulated all the students who tried and started recording their times on the score sheet. The class was about to end.

Suddenly, Mr. Hunt realized that not all his students were in line as they were walking into the gym. Out of a 40-minute class, those girls had so little drive that they couldn't make it through the mile run before the class was going back to the classroom. These girls had no motivation.

Obstacle

How to inspire the unmotivated runners.

Common Mistake

Giving up on lazy runners.

Solutions

- Talk to the unmotivated students privately. Explain what they should be capable of and the time frame that they should be able to run within. They may pull through, but you can't give up.

- The very next day, have the students who didn't try run again. You are only doing it for their benefit. This will benefit them by improving not only their score, but their health.

If they still can't improve after the above ideas, have them run at least a half-mile for their warm-up each day, while the others are doing a fun tag warm-up. This is not to be a punishment, but rather a method to help the students in poor shape improve their cardiovascular fitness and stamina. We are not using running as a punishment, at all, we are using it as a tool to improve students' cardiovascular fitness levels and overall health. Stress to the student this fact and why this plan is being followed. After all, that is one of the reasons we have physical education.

Retest the students after doing the above. They will improve! Also give students very positive feedback. Make them feel good about their accomplishments. Tell them how good it is for them physically and mentally.

Tip

> If you have a very stubborn, lazy, or unmotivated student, call the child's home. Ask the parents if there is a medical reason that their child is doing so poorly on the fitness test. If they are cleared of any medical condition, retest them, with much encouragement. If there is a medical concern, then you'll need to find out if it is a temporary condition, or one that will require you to give an alternate, adapted physical test. There should be an alternate for those students with disabilities. The President's Physical Fitness Challenge offers opportunities and standards for those students. Check out the pamphlet for the President's Physical Fitness Challenge.

Real-Life Story

Four fifth-grade girls were acting as if they didn't care and were walking and talking through the mile run. The physical education teacher called each parent, with the student present, and asked if there was a medical reason for them to be this slow. The teacher discussed their attitude with the parents, too. Lo and behold, the next day the 40-minute mile run turned into a 10-minute national award score. This is the power of parents knowing what their children are trying to get away with!

NAME	SCORE	RECORD	COMMENTS
MICHAEL JOHNSON	3.02 min/sec	YES	FASTEST MILE TIME
GLORIA BUTLER	8:09 min/sec	NO	1'
SUSAN TAYLOR	40:00 min/sec	YES	SLOWEST MILE SCORE EVER RECORDED

"YIKES! THE BALL HIT ME!"

On a rainy day, 150 students were crammed into the tiny gym. The students had the choice of playing either volleyball or basketball. Some students were playing vigorously, some were playing for fun, and some were standing out there just to keep from getting a zero for the day. All the physical education teachers were huddled together, generally not paying attention to the 150 sixth-graders for whom they were responsible.

Tamisha was on the volleyball court, not playing, just standing on it and talking. Suddenly, a ball flew across the net and smacked her in the head. Luckily, she wasn't hurt. She said, "Yikes! The ball hit me! Who hit that ball that hit me?" She was trying to blame someone who was doing the right thing in physical education class, when she was obviously wrong for standing in the middle of the volleyball game.

That's what happens when students are doing nothing but socializing during physical education.

Obstacle

> Dealing with the students who try to get away with doing nothing in physical education.

Common Mistake

> Letting students get away with being a "slacker."

Solutions

- Don't ignore it. Slackness is contagious!
- If a student has the potential to be a "slacker," give her a lot of positive feedback.
- Students will enjoy the positive attention so much that they will want to participate in order to get that positive feedback from you.
- Stay on those students! Never give up. Somebody at home already might have.
- Keep in close proximity of these students, and keep them moving.

Tip

> Students who are allowed to slack will slowly wreck your class. Take care of the problem now before the class loses its energy.

Real-Life Story 📖

Unfortunately, Ms. Vaughn was doing her student teaching at Kempton High School when she witnessed Tamisha and the ball incident. Tamisha had the attitude that nobody should "dare" get a ball near her regardless of the fact that she was standing idle in the middle of the volleyball court when she was supposed to be participating. Ms. Vaughn will never forget the situation she witnessed. What made it worse was that this was supposed to be a learning experience, in order to entice potential physical education majors to pursue a career in teaching physical education. Fortunately, Ms. Vaughn used this experience as the fire to push her to get her degree and teaching license. She wanted to change the apathetic programs that might be out there in physical education. Now she is supervising physical education teachers and making sure that no teachers are as poor as the ones that she had witnessed.

YELLOW SHOELACES

"Can you tie my shoe, please?" We hear that question over and over. Beware before you act. Some teachers like to tie the kindergartners' and first-graders' shoes, while others think they should learn how to tie their own shoes.

Beware? The request seems innocent enough. So, you look down at the student's feet and you tie the shoes. No problem. What is so hard about that?

The other students notice that you are tying shoes, so they come running over to ask you to do the honors for them, too. So, you keep on looping and circling and pulling the laces. You are trying to speed up the process, and you just tie and tie, one shoe after another. You aren't listening to the students because you assume they are all saying, "Can you tie my shoes, too?"

However, one student wasn't asking for his shoes to be tied. You figure this out not because you were listening, but as you are working on the shoe assembly line, a first-grader's shoelaces suddenly turn from bright white to a pretty shade of soggy yellow. That's right—beware of the yellow shoelaces!

Excitement and movement are a combination that seems to make kids have to go to the bathroom immediately.

Obstacle

What do you do when a student has to go to the bathroom?

Common Mistakes

- Allowing students to go to the bathroom whenever they want.
- Not allowing students to go, thus changing the color of their shoelaces from white to soggy yellow—and yellow shoelaces may be only one part of a string of other problems.

Solutions

- Establish rules for safety at the very beginning of the school year. Make a rule that the time is so valuable that the class can't afford to lose the time to go to the bathroom. The students don't want to miss physical education so giving them this responsibility is sensible and vital.
- Ask the classroom teachers to permit students to go to the bathroom before coming to PE class.
- Explain the importance of not leaving the teacher's sight. Students shouldn't go from way out in the field to inside of a

building, where they are many yards away from the supervising teacher, or go where no one is supervising.

Tips 🏃

- Stick to your rules—however, don't be inhuman! You know how it feels when you really have to go. Use your best judgment. When a student comes up to you and is dancing, grabbing his crotch, crying, and crossing his legs, he is in trouble. Let him go! He is not playing around. If you don't, you'll not only have yellow shoelaces, but pile on to that a wet gym or field, wet equipment, an embarrassed student, and having to call in the cleanup crew to start the disinfection process.
- Review your rules every month. It's worth the minute of talking. Also, politely remind all teachers to let students go to the bathroom before physical education class.

Real-Life Story 📖

Stuart had to go to the bathroom, so Mrs. Polk let him go. Immediately after he took his first step toward the bathroom, 10 other students also had to go. The students hollered out and raised their hands, so Mrs. Polk was bombarded by anxious requests and had to let all 10 go out of fairness. Mrs. Polk now lost at least 10 minutes of instructional time, as well as the attention of 10 students.

EXCUSES, EXCUSES, EXCUSES

"My throat hurts."

"I have a sunburn."

"My ankle is sore."

"I'm wearing a dress."

"My mom told me to take it easy today. It hurts when I use this arm."

"My stomach aches."

"I can't run today because I had soccer practice last night, and I'm worn out."

"I forgot my shoes."

"I can't do jumping jacks because it makes me jiggle too much, and it hurts."

"I just can't run because it always hurts some part of me."

"My legs are too short to do well on the V-sit test."

"He can do pull-ups because he's skinny, but I've got a lot of muscle in my legs and everyone knows that muscles weigh a lot."

"I can't because I'm not allowed to get dirty."

These are only a few of the many excuses students come up with in order to not participate in physical education. You'll have to listen to them all—some will be valid and others will make a student's nose grow. You'll have to weed through the fakers and bellyachers and know the difference between these and the real concerns.

You will *always* have someone who will complain for attention. But you need to take a look at your physical education program if you keep getting a lot of excuses and notes from the students. Why are so many students trying to get out of class?

Obstacle

How do you stop the students from feeding you a lot of excuses?

Common Mistakes

- Blaming the students for being "weaklings."
- Not searching for the real reason.
- Not listening.
- Allowing the complainers to continue to complain and find weak excuses.

Solutions

Search for the underlying problem. Why don't the students want to participate? They probably are making these excuses because they don't want to do what you have planned for them. Saying they are sick gives them an excuse to not have to perform for you.

Are your lessons repetitive and monotonous? Make a change. Don't have them run a lap every single day. Change it to warm-ups such as tag, sprints, a quarter-mile jog, running while dribbling for a quarter-mile, or exercising with "Exer-dice":

Have the students roll dice and then perform the exercise that matches up with the number rolled. This is also a good interlinking activity. Interlinking incorporates physical education with core subjects such as math, language arts, science, and social studies. Try these rules:

- Roll a 2, do 30 jumping jacks.
- Roll a 3, do one lap around a squared-off boundary.
- Roll a 4, sprint to the wall and back.
- Roll a 5, do 30 arm circles each way.
- Roll a 6, do 30 heel raises.
- Roll a 7, perform 20-second inside hurdle stretch.
- Roll an 8, do 20 push-ups.
- Roll a 9, do 30 crunches.
- Roll a 10, do 30 twists.
- Roll an 11, do 10 cheerleader jumps.
- Roll a 12, take your choice.

Are the students intimidated? Are they afraid of others laughing at them? You need to create an environment in which all students can't wait to come to PE class. Do not let students make others feel bad.

If students are complaining for attention, quiet them as quickly as you can. Hear them out and then explain the procedures for being excused from physical activity. Let them know that you are concerned about them; however, the problem has to be legitimate to tell the teacher. Describe a legitimate concern: a broken leg, recovering from pneumonia, or having a parent's or doctor's note. If a student ever has an emergency or illness that requires a nurse's attention, this would be a time to tell the teacher about the concern.

Tips

- Make your lessons so exciting that no one ever wants to miss out on a single lesson. Do you have any excuses on Field Day? The physical education teachers that I know have no notes to excuse students from Field Day. On the contrary, the teachers get notes from parents asking them to please allow their children to participate in whatever possible, even though the student may have a broken arm. Why? Because students love Field Day.

- If a student sits out, make the experience one that he doesn't enjoy, so that he can't wait to get back in.

Real-Life Story

When Roberta came to physical education class, she immediately approached the instructor with a concern about a pain that hurt so much that she couldn't possibly participate. She was a complainer who hated to run. The teacher was hip to her game and said, "You can sit out, but next time you'll need a note." The instructor knew that Roberta thought that today was a running day, because she had been peeking through her class window earlier in the day, curious to see what was happening in PE class. The instructor had caught on to this trend, because she could see students looking out, trying to see what fun things were happening in PE. The instructor threw everyone off guard by changing the plan. She organized a fun game that day that she knew Roberta would love to play. In this way, Roberta could not assume that the class would be doing a particular activity, so from then on, she hesitated about complaining.

FIGHTING OVER FAVORS

Teaching can be great, especially teaching physical education. The students want to please you so much. But did you ever think that students would get into fights over doing favors? Well, Mrs. Peters soon discovered that she couldn't take her eyes off of the students, even the ones who begged to be her helping assistant. You're probably thinking, *How in the world can offering to help you be a problem?* It's how you handle it that's the potential problem.

Obstacle

Letting students help you.

Common Mistake

Assuming that the students can be left alone, just because they are volunteering to do a good deed.

Solutions

- If someone asks to help, give her easy, specific directions.
- Keep your eyes on your students while they help. If it is to deliver a message, then only choose a person with a reliable track record that you can trust to make the delivery successful.
- Do the task yourself if you have any doubts about the capabilities of a student messenger.
- Use designated physical education helpers to set up and break down, with your direct supervision.
- Praise students for their volunteering.

Tips

- Remember the "back to the wall" strategy of teaching. Keep all the children within view by standing so that no student can get behind your back. (see more on the subject in "Don't Turn Your Back" in chapter 12).
- You are responsible for anything that happens while those students are working for you.
- Use your best, reasonable, and fair judgment.
- Remember to offer praise to students for their effort.

Real-Life Story

Mrs. Peters had allowed Tyrone and Terrance to put away her equipment after class. They raced over to the balls and cones and started their task. Then Tyrone decided that he should be in charge of the balls, since he started collecting them first. Terrance didn't share that same logic. So then the two began tugging balls back and forth, and the yelling began. The yelling turned into ball throwing, which turned into beaning each other with the balls, which turned into pushing each other, then punching each other—all over doing the teacher a favor.

Mrs. Peters, unfortunately, did not practice the "back to the wall" strategy and by the time she saw them they were pushing and punching. Mission was not accomplished. Not only did the equipment not get picked up, but it also caused her more work and embarrassment. The two terror volunteers spent the next day at home, suspended because of fighting over doing a favor for the teacher.

NATURAL NOISES

Our bodies can make some noises that can make everyone laugh or cry, come to us or run away. Physical education makes our bodies exert, so some surprising and sometimes unwanted actions occur.

Sometimes we breathe heavily when we run. Moving makes us perspire and, thus, smell not so good. Sweat makes us wet. When hitting a tennis ball with all your might, you may let out a big grunt. Going above and beyond to exceed a goal sometimes makes us groan. But the noise that naturally comes from the body, without conscious effort, is the release of air that has to come out. You may have heard of the huge belchers who can belt one loud enough to hear it "in the next city." When kids are swimming, this burping instinct takes over.

Another exercise causes a release of air, but from another part of our bodies: the passing of gas through the gluteus maximus muscles. The exercises that really contribute to this are the abdominal exercises— sit-ups, curl-ups, and crunches. Beware, during physical fitness testing, when the students are vigorously pushing out some curl-ups, they might accidentally push out some extra wind. The person holding the feet should watch out, because he is right in the target zone.

Obstacle

Getting through the laughter, embarrassment, and smell of the accidental breaking of wind.

Common Mistakes

- Making a face or turning up their nose.
- Embarrassing the student further.

Solutions

- Use the teachable moment when it occurs. Tell the students that passing gas is as natural as breathing—if it happens to someone, it's normal and natural, so there's no need to laugh at him.
- Explain that performing curl-ups, or anything that requires pushing of the stomach muscles, could cause this reaction, so students should be prepared.

Tips

- Tell the students to beware when holding the feet of someone doing curl-ups. If that person breaks wind, they only have to hold their breath for a few seconds.

- Explain that when performing curl-ups, students should not stop if the wind breaks loose. Tell them to keep going!
- Another suggestion: not laughing, because that uses one's abdominals.

Real-Life Story

During a curl-up test, Jim was holding Tom's feet when suddenly Tom passed gas! It was so loud that Jim let go of Tom's feet, flung himself backward to get away, and hit the wall with his head. Tom kept on going. Tom got a good score in the curl-ups and Jim went to the nurse to get ice on his head.

"HE SAID ..."

"He looked at me."

"She said that I was dumb."

"He said that my mom was fat."

"He said that I catch like a girl."

"She said that I can't get my spot back in line now."

Tattletales! What would school be like if we had no tattletales? It must be a natural instinct for some children. Some of them just love to tattle. This little habit will wear on your nerves, so nip it now!

Obstacle

How do you stop the tattletales?

Common Mistakes

- Mistaking an important comment from a habitual tattletale as unimportant.
- Saying something like, "Only come up to me if you are bleeding, vomiting, or dying"—which makes you very unapproachable.

Solutions

- Discuss tattling: telling on someone when you should just ignore the person. Tell the class that some children say things that aren't true because they feel bad about themselves. Others say things that aren't true to get someone upset. And still others say things because they want attention.
- Tell the class that there is a time to tell a teacher and there are times when students must wait. If a teacher is in the middle of instruction, they should not approach and interrupt!
- Give students examples of when they should tell or interrupt:

    If someone has an emergency.

    If there is a strange occurrence (e.g., a stranger entering).

    If a ball is about to hit someone.

    If someone is threatening someone else.

If a person is offending someone by actions or improper language.

If someone is being hurt.

- Tell the students that it is tattling when they tell on someone who says something that is not correct. It is not true, so they shouldn't let it bother them. For example, if someone calls them a dog, it isn't true, so why let it bother them?

Tip

Tell the story about the boy who "cried wolf."

Real-Life Story

Donatella always tattled in the classroom. The kids all called her a tattletale. The students in the class started to ignore her and not speak to her. She soon realized that she wasn't liked because of her tattling. She went to the physical education teacher and said, "No one likes to work with me because I'm a tattletale." That battle was easy to solve, because it solved itself. The kids watched what they did, so they didn't get ratted on, assuming that Donatella would tell. Donatella worked on stopping the tattling so that people would like her more.

LINE LEADER

The first person in a race gets an award. The first-place team gets a trophy. The first-place Olympian gets a gold medal. The first person to discover or invent something gets recognition. The first-place tennis player wins money. So it's easily understood why students would want to be first in a sport. Who wouldn't?

What is the prize for being first in line? Why do students always seem to want to be first in line? Because they get the best view of the school? Because they want to be the first one to enter their classroom? Because then they don't have to stare at the person's head in front of them? The students have assigned seats in the classroom, so it's not as if they won't get a seat. First, or last, they'll still get to their desk. Some students also get upset and tattle about others cutting in line. A student could be the 22nd person out of 25 and still get upset if someone tried to get in line in front of her. Students worry too much about the line.

Obstacle

Getting students not to worry about where they are in line.

Common Mistake

Not paying attention to your line.

Solutions

Make it a point to discuss the matter of line leader at the beginning of the school year. Mention the following to the class:

- They all will get where they are going no matter where they are in line.
- There's no prize for the line leader.
- The line leader doesn't get to pick first.
- Line placement is insignificant. (Make sure that you're not causing the students to worry about line placement because of the way you are distributing equipment.)

Give out the equipment in different patterns. Try these rules:

- The second-to-the-last person in line can get his ball and choose his partner first.
- Students wearing green can form a circle.
- The person who has a birthday in December can get her equipment.
- The people that you point to may line up. (This is my favorite, because it ensures that they are paying attention and totally focusing on you. It's a good method for eye contact.)
- Numbers are picked at random, for lining up or getting equipment.
- Anyone fighting or arguing over the line goes to the end. If two students are fighting over a spot in line, neither student is allowed to get that spot. They must go to the end to pick last and get out of the way of the others, who are in line following directions.

Tip

Have a line-leader game: Everyone gets in line, and then you call a number out at random. That number in line gets to earn a choice. He may be able to pick first, choose the exercise of the day, be the teacher's helper, and so forth. However, the student at the front of line is always excluded. You can explain this to the students as they play the game. If you find that no one wants to lead the line, then you've succeeded, and they can stop playing the game.

Real-Life Story

Kooky as it may seem, most of the problems and fussing don't come from physical activity, but from a line concern. Alex and Bart were gently nudging each other in line. Each nudge became stronger and the nudges turned into pushes. Alex decided to give Bart a big push, because he didn't want Bart to get in front of him. Bart responded with a double-handed, stronger push, because he thought it was wrong of Alex to push him like that. Alex got angry and threw a punch at Bart, which made Bart's nose bleed and fueled the fire in

Bart to punch Alex in revenge. Bart and Alex wound up first in line—
to the principal's office, that is. Students have gotten themselves
suspended because the nudging turns to pushing, and the pushing
turns into a fight. It sounds pretty silly for a student to tell his parents
that he got suspended because he was fighting over being 15th in line
and the other person almost made him the 16th. This happens with
adults, too—so let's prevent it now.

"OUCH!"

"Ms. Stone, I think Bobby is broken," a worried little girl says as she runs up to "save" Bobby. Ms. Stone knows that Bobby always is trying to get attention by staying on the ground for extended periods of time—like the NBA players when they make a slight tap turn into a tackle, tumble, and roll. Nevertheless, Ms. Stone has to acknowledge the girl's information.

Sometimes there will be fakers, and sometimes, unfortunately, there will be real injuries. That's just what comes with the territory of physical activity. A quality physical education teacher, fortunately, can greatly minimize the real injuries through careful planning, reasonable thinking, and good judgment.

Obstacle

Handling injuries correctly.

Common Mistakes

- Being negligent in planning.
- Being negligent in supervision.

Solutions

- Make lesson plans with the students in mind. Think about the following:

    Age—is the activity geared toward this age level?

    Skill level—are the students ready, or mature enough, to handle the skill you want them to learn?

    Experience—have they done this skill before?

    Space—is the space adequate? (See the safety space chart.)

    Interest—will the students be bored with an unchallenging lesson? If so, they will try to overcome the boredom by creating new and challenging ways of doing your lesson.

- Make sure you pay attention to injuries, no matter how small, and determine whether the student should see the nurse.

- If the student is a habitual faker, speak to her about "crying wolf" and talk to the class afterward about helping others when necessary and leaving alone those who cry wolf.

- Be sure you have current CPR and first aid training. You can call your local American Red Cross chapter for classes.

Table 3.1   **Safety Spaces**

Activity	Distance from other students	Distance from building Partner #1	Distance from building Partner #2
Throwing	10 feet	30 feet	50 feet
Kicking	15 feet	30 feet	50 feet
Punting	20 feet	30 feet	50 feet
Striking with rackets	15 feet	30 feet	50 feet
Striking with hockey sticks	15 feet	30 feet	50 feet
Striking with golf clubs	20 feet	30 feet	50 feet
Dribbling with sticks	*3 feet personal space, although sticks may touch	30 feet	50 feet
Throwing with lacrosse sticks	15 feet	30 feet	50 feet

Distance will vary with each grade level

- Carry the following items with you at all times: gloves, bandages, and pen and paper. These fit easily inside box clipboards or small pouches.
- Call a student's home when an accident has happened, to stay in communication with his parents.
- Double-check the safety checklist (located on next page).

Tip

You've heard it before—"an ounce of prevention is worth a pound of cure." How true. Check yourself before doing any and every lesson, by making sure safety always is taken into consideration. You'll be happy you did.

Real-Life Story

During an activity in which students were going through an obstacle course, attempting to avoid being hit by a thrown foam ball, George knocked out a tooth. The next day, his parents were in the principal's office, trying to blame the school and talking about possibly suing. The physical education teacher had checked the age level, skill level, space, experience, interest level, and gym, and all met the necessary specifications for a good, safe lesson on fitness, locomotor movements, and throwing at a moving target. The reason George knocked out his tooth was because he didn't follow directions, and he simply

Table 3.2 **Injury Checklist**

Injury	Ask student	Ask nurse	Call parent	Call EMS	No participation
Scrape	X	If needing more than a bandage			
Cut	X	If needing peroxide or stitches	If needing more than a bandage		Student/teacher determination
Strain	X	Swelling, discomfort	Nurse may call		Student/teacher determination
Sprain	X	X	X		X
Fracture	X	X	X	X, unless the parents alter	X
Dizziness	X	X	X	X, depends on circumstances	X
Student with note about an illness	X				X
Student is complaining with no note or call	X	See if student has seen nurse	Depends on circumstances		X
Fainting	X	X	X	X	X
Asthma	X	See if student has seen nurse	Nurse may call	Rarely	Student/teacher determination
Collisions	X	If bumps arise, or to the head, or bleeding	Nurse may call	Rarely	Student/teacher determination
Nosebleed	X	X	Nurse may call		
Heat injury	X	If genuine	X	Rarely	Student/teacher determination
Cold injury	X				
Bites	X	Ask if allergic	Nurse may call	Rarely	

ran into a boy in front of him. The boy in front was fine, and he must have had a hard head, because George cracked his tooth by bumping into his head. The other students had no trouble with any injuries. Once George's parents realized that this was an accident, purely caused by their son's own negligence, they backed down and left the school alone.

4

"IT'S PHYSICAL EDUCATION TIME!"

"WHAT ARE WE DOING IN PE TODAY?"

Here comes Mr. Jones' class for physical education. As the students approach the gym, they can hardly hold back. It's like a horse at the starting gate, anxiously waiting for it to spring open, so it can be free and run. As the students cross the threshold of the gym doors, their eyes light up, their smiles greet you, and one familiar phrase passes from their lips for you to hear: "What are we doing in PE today?"

Throughout the day, the students have peeked down the hall to sneak a preview of what they will get to do in physical education class, their favorite class. Even though it's now their time to participate, they still cannot wait to find out what adventure is in store for them today. They even will start guessing: "I hope it's soccer today." "No, it's got to be running." "No, I think it's the parachute." Then they start looking for evidence of what the activity might be: "If they have the slips of paper, it must be running club," because slips of paper are used to keep track of laps. Or, "If she's got the bullhorn it must be grand centers," because the students are to switch from center to center on the bullhorn's signal.

Should we be concerned about this constant investigating and questioning? We should be concerned if they are *not* asking.

Obstacle

> Your students keep asking you that same question: "What are we doing in PE today?"

Common Mistakes

- Shouting back at them to be quiet.
- Saying, "Don't ask me that question."
- Squashing their enthusiasm!

Solutions

- Have patience, even though the students don't.
- Understand their excitement, and keep them guessing. Egg them on to figuring out what the activity might be. This is a lot of fun, and it builds the excitement that physical education brings to the students anyway.
- Tell them, "I can't wait to tell you, but let's hold off until we are in our huddle." Tell them each day what they will be doing only when they are in a huddle in front of you with eager ears to listen. Keep this consistent. Don't tell one student before the others; otherwise they'll come up to you one at a time and question you.

Tips

- Start the school year off by explaining the procedure of learning the day's activity in the huddle.
- Imagine that your activity is a wrapped present that you are giving to the students each day. That's how they see physical education—as a gift given by the school that they can't wait to tear the paper off and play with.
- If the questions get out of hand in the middle of the year, repeat the explanation and procedures.
- The biggest thing to remember about the never-ending question of "What are we doing in PE today?" is to be thrilled that they are excited enough to wonder and ask.

Real-Life Story

The students were always so excited to find out what we were going to do each day that I decided to make it a contest. The student who didn't shout out but waited until we got into our huddle and raised his hand was the one able to ask the question and also suggest what he thought we were doing. This was very rewarding for the student. Other students wanted to do this, day after day. This also can give you ideas of activities.

45 MINUTES AND "OFF YOU GO"

Students sit, listen, learn, write, read, compute, and concentrate for six hours a day. That means that Brandon, the ball-hog "bully," stays with his elementary school homeroom teacher every minute except for physical education, lunch, art, music, and computer. That's a very long time to have to deal with behavior problems of a classroom bully. Brandon's teacher also has other students whom she must manage carefully, and discipline, throughout the day.

As physical education teachers, we are sitting pretty! We only see students for about 45 minutes at a time. Some of us see them five days a week, while others see them once a week. We have fun with them, enjoy them, while they enjoy us temporarily, and then we send them off to their classroom teacher again.

This may seem ideal for the behavior problems, but what about the other concerns this presents?

Obstacles

- Forty-five minutes is not enough time to cover everything that you need to cover.
- Students only have physical education once a week—how can anything be accomplished?
- Your students may have to change clothes, which only leaves them with a solid 25 minutes for physical education.
- Students may have to choose among chorus, strings, newspaper, and other special classes on physical education days.

Common Mistake

Complaining about the time with which you are given to work.

Solutions

- Make the most of every single second that you have the students.
- Grin and bear it for those few 45 minutes that you have a behavior problem.

Tips

- For those 45 minutes that you have the class, make the time so valuable to your students that the teachers, the principal, and, of course, the students realize the importance of your program.

- If physical education class is considered a valuable and needed use of time, you could be earning your program more time in the future of physical education at your school.

- The class bully will want to behave for you because he knows that he only has 45 minutes to participate in physical education. He won't want to ruin that by sitting in "time out" for poor behavior!

Real-Life Story

In one private school that demanded that all students change into shorts, shirt, socks, and tennis shoes for physical education, the lack-of-time dilemma was encountered. The students had physical education twice a week for 45 minutes. Changing clothes decreased the total teaching time from 90 possible minutes to 50 minutes. It was proven to the principal, teachers, and students that this physical education program was worthwhile! The following year, PE was increased by one day and instead of the physical education teacher getting the students to change, the classroom teacher would bring them fully ready to participate! The total possible teaching time increased dramatically.

"I GOT AN 'A' IN PHYSICAL EDUCATION"

How does a student get an "A" in physical education? Better yet, how does one not get an "A"? Grading in physical education can be tricky. Do you give students who can run fast and are great athletes the good grades, and the not-so-good students the poor grades? Some students fail physical education somehow.

Do people really care about what grade they get in physical education? Should there be grades in physical education? On what are the students graded? Should students be held back for failing physical education? Do parents get angry if their child fails physical education, or do they shake it off as a joke? Do the parents get angry at you for failing their child in physical education? No one should fail physical education. We should set students up to excel in physical education, not fail.

Obstacle

How do you grade students?

Common Mistakes

- Grading on athletic ability.
- Grading solely on dressing for physical education—students learn how to dress at home, so it's not good to give them a poor grade for not changing correctly.

Solutions

- Think about whether you want to place a lot of emphasis on grading. It may be better to de-emphasize grades and just concentrate on participating and performing—especially at the elementary school level. You can give a grade, but don't make it a major focus of the program.
- Have a grading design. Calculate what percentage is based on performance versus behavior. Do you want to separate the behavior grade from the performance grade? Figure out how much weight to place on assessment.
- Remember that your field is not weighed as heavily as math, English, or science, so don't get aggravated and make it hard on yourself.

- Make your assessments simple to grade.
- Design a grading system. Explain it to your students, as well as to their parents in a letter. Here's a sample:

Grade	Participation	Assessment Marks	Behavior Marks	Proper Uniform
A	100%	3 outstanding	3 outstanding	100%
B	100%	1 outstanding	2 outstanding	95%
C	95%	at least satisfactory	at least satisfactory	90%
D	85%	less than satisfactory	3 poor marks	80%
F	<85%	over 3 poor marks	over 3 poor marks	<80%

- See if you and your principal can work out a method for those students who do not dress properly, without displaying the "not dressing" grade on the report card. It is futile to make the whole grade about dressing. Grades are fine if they have good value. Make sure that your grades reflect what you want them to reflect.

Tip

Try hard to encourage the students to earn an "A" in physical education and heavily discourage them to ever receive an "F." Let them know that there is absolutely no reason to get a poor grade.

Real-Life Story

Tony had not dressed properly for physical education for a month. He loved to participate and was a great athlete. He was getting an "F" in physical education, however, because the rule was that if a student didn't change into a physical education uniform, he couldn't participate. If he couldn't participate, he couldn't get good participation marks or any assessment marks. He is doomed to a bad grade. It turned out that Tony's uniform was stolen and his parents couldn't afford to buy another one. So, his parents chose to feed him rather than buy another physical education uniform, and they chose to brush off the physical education grade, because it wasn't as important to them. They knew their son was a good student and good at physical skills. So, make sure you investigate certain issues, such as this one, before it is too late.

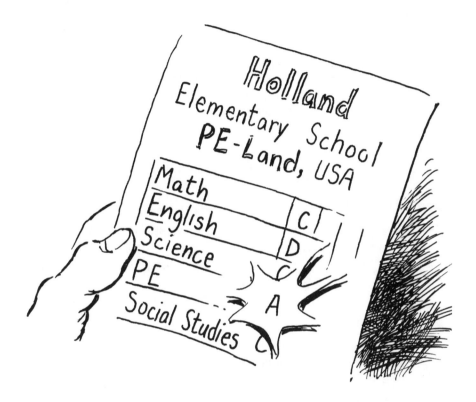

RECESS RULES

"Out of control"—those are the best words to describe recess. Often, it is an accident waiting to happen at recess time. Unfortunately, people try to link recess with physical education. Just because they are both done outside, and involve playing, doesn't mean they are the same.

Baseball bats are swinging, students are not being supervised, and you are watching the potential fiasco from a distance as you teach your structured physical education class. The classroom teacher is diligently working to grade papers, as she stands her watch on recess duty. Meanwhile, the students have a heyday. All kinds of physical education rules are being broken. Help!

Obstacle

Trying to distinguish physical education from recess.

Common Mistakes

- Creating a program in which teachers, students, and parents can't tell the difference between physical education and recess
- Conducting a program in which the students prefer recess over physical education

Solutions

- Create a solid, worthwhile program in which every single lesson has an objective, creates a sense of accomplishment for the students, and is fun.
- If you make the learning of skills too much like "boot camp," the students will prefer recess over physical education.
- Alert the principal, immediately, of potential dangers such as safety hazards on the playground and fields and the negligent actions of students or others.
- Conduct a seminar for teachers on inappropriate play on the playground at recess. Give them some advice and let them know the safety practices you insist upon in physical education class. Give them a list of "no-no's":

    No bats

    No tackling

    No tumbling

    No behavior at recess that would not be accepted in physical education

No recess unless the teacher is able to watch and supervise the students

No grading papers

Tip

Make it perfectly clear to your students that there is a difference between physical education and recess. Physical education is structured and should be informative while involving the students in engaging activities to support the objectives. Recess is unstructured and should allow the students the freedom to choose their own activities to participate in. Then have them live the difference.

Real-Life Story

Recess became mandatory at Hudgins Elementary School. This greatly increased the school nurse's patient numbers. The nurse became so concerned that she asked for a seminar for the teachers on safe recess behavior.

chapter

5

TOOLS
OF THE TRADE

"PRETEND THIS IS A ..."

Remember when you were a kid and you would pretend that one of your toys was real? Or when you played with Barbie, Ken, or GI Joe and imagined that they were real people and gave them the appropriate names?

Some physical education teachers will get lucky and have a large amount of physical education equipment. Even those people always want more. Some teachers will struggle with bits and pieces of equipment.

With a lot of imagination, and positive thinking, you can make a bean bag turn into a shot put, a ball, a piece of food, a base, or anything else.

Obstacle

Not having the equipment you need for the skills you are teaching.

Common Mistake

Omitting skills and activities because you don't have the proper equipment.

Solutions

- Don't be narrow-minded. Use your imagination.
- You could use the following for the real deal:

    Use a lummi stick, or the 8-inch cylindrical rods called rhythm sticks, for a track baton.

    A ball of used floor tape collected over time can become a shot put.

    Tape over a Frisbee to make a discus.

    Stretch a rope to serve as a tennis or volleyball net.

    Raise a Hula Hoop to become a basketball rim.

    Milk jugs with the bottom cut out become scoops.

    Look at cones and rope and imagine hurdles.

    Steps or risers can be steps for step aerobics.

    Carpet squares can be bases, markers, or boundaries.

    Large traffic cones are batting tees.

Socks balled up and tied are soft balls.

A tennis ball in a sock is an easy tracker ball, for students in lower grades to track the ball and catch the tail, if not the ball section.

Tip

If you can pretend, you will enjoy your lessons, as if you were a kid again. When you pretend, the students get into the lesson even more!

Real-Life Story

Mrs. Lambden wanted to do a track unit to expose her students to the fun and excitement of track-and-field events. She used makeshift equipment for just about everything. The students still appreciated it and got a great experience, regardless of doing most of the events with pretend equipment.

BUDGET? WHAT BUDGET?

"Yes, I'm definitely interested in the job!" says the excited physical education teacher candidate. Then she starts asking questions: "Where's the gym?" "How much money do I have to spend on equipment?" "How often can we afford to buy new equipment?"

Some schools don't have a large physical education budget. And sometimes there is no budget at all! But don't panic—there are other means of getting equipment. Just be glad that the school has found the money to pay a physical education teacher.

Obstacle

How to work with skills that require equipment when you don't have a budget for equipment.

Common Mistake

Limiting your program to certain activities just because you lack specific equipment.

Solutions

- Improvise.
- Have other means to get equipment. You truly can get a lot of equipment without putting out any money! Examples: a Campbell's soup labels collecting program, a cereal box tops collecting program, or proof-of-purchase programs from food distributors. Here are some contacts:

    Labels for education—**www.labelsforeducation.com**

    General Mills box tops for education—**www.boxtops4education.com**

    Hershey's fund-raising—**www.hersheys.com**

- Try other fund-raising ideas:

    A turkey trot, a jingle bell jog, or a spring run—in which entries to compete cost a minimal charge.

    Sponsoring drives or competitions—such as a free-throw competition, in which sponsors pay a set amount or pay by accomplishment of the activity.

Sales of T-shirts, school supplies, or novelty items with profits going to the physical education budget—a great way to raise money as well as promote school spirit.

An auction.

Magazine or candy drives—but make sure the rules secure the students' safety.

- Ask for donations of equipment that people are no longer using. It may take time, but you will gain inventory through the years.

- Ask a local college to keep your school in its thoughts when it gets rid of old equipment.

- Of course, try to prove to your principal that physical education is important and slowly work physical education into the pages of the budget report. Prove physical education's value by conducting worthwhile classes and promoting your subject, and then the students will promote your subject to their parents, who will communicate it to the principal.

Tips

- Get excited about fund-raising! It's rewarding and fun.
- Make sure to promptly thank those who donate to you.
- Take good care of your equipment. Instill in the students' minds the importance of taking care of what they have.

Real-Life Story

The Campbell's soup label drive was a phenomenal success at one elementary school. This was the only way that the school had received equipment in the past. The teacher made the collection process a competition—the class that collected the most labels at the end of the year would receive a pizza and ice cream party. This school collected thousands and thousands of labels. By the end of the year, the school got 10 playground balls, 10 basketballs, 10 footballs, 10 jump ropes, 10 Hula Hoops, 10 bats, 10 softballs, and a rack for the equipment. This was fun, rewarding, and free to the school, except for the party. The Campbell's labels for education program is great. Check it out!

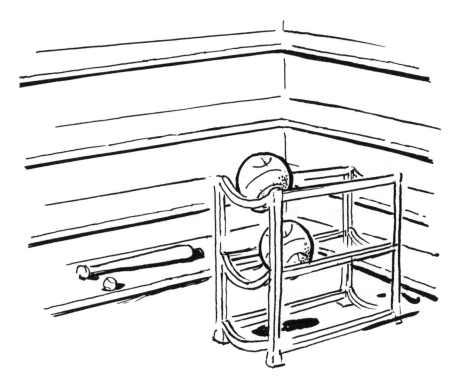

EQUIPMENT SANTA

When people need to get a book, read a newspaper, or research something, where do they go? The library. When students want to play with some equipment at school, they go to the person who has all the equipment: you, the physical education teacher.

First someone asks to borrow a playground ball. Then a classroom teacher sends a student to get a football for their class, during the middle of the physical education class. You can't stop the instruction to get equipment, and you don't want to send in the student alone to get the equipment. The teachers then ask to borrow Hula Hoops, jump ropes, and a few balls for their recess throughout the year. They come to you at all different times and ask you to stock their wish list with some of your equipment. You've become the equipment Santa.

Obstacle

How to handle the wish list of classroom teachers who want to borrow your equipment.

Common Mistakes

- Letting everyone borrow whatever they want.
- Being the "Grinch."

Solutions

- Be helpful to teachers when they want to borrow equipment that supports and reinforces their lessons. Beware, however—once you start catering to the requests of others, the requests will increase.
- Establish guidelines for lending equipment. Turnaround time should be one week, and teachers cannot borrow items that you will be using—physical education comes first. Have the teachers fill out a form and submit it to you. The form should have the following information:

  Date of request

  Teacher's name

  Quantity

  How long the equipment is needed

Table 5.1 **Physical Education Equipment Checkout**

Date Requested: _____
(Give as much advance notice as possible)

Date Needed: _____
(No more than one week in duration)

Name: _____

Item: _____

How Many: _____

Teacher's Signature: _____

Physical Education Teacher: _____

- Request a pack of equipment for each grade level for recess. Let the classroom teachers have the responsibility for the equipment. They can use this whenever they want, and they won't have to come to you. Make sure you order it for them. This will ensure that they get age-appropriate and safe equipment. Some ideas for the recess pack:

    One playground ball for every six kids

    One basketball

    Six jump ropes

    Two long or double ropes

    Six hula hoops

    Four foam balls

    One foam football

    One foam Frisbee disc

- Make sure you get durable equipment. And color coding is a good idea.

Tip

Do this at the beginning of the year!

Real-Life Story

Recess is required in some schools. A typical recess would find many students standing around gossiping, doing nothing, getting themselves into trouble, or fighting over the one playground ball. So instead of students standing around doing nothing, with nothing, the principal and the physical education teacher at Dutch Elementary School ordered equipment for each grade level. Since balls are always in demand, there were enough that there was no more fighting over the single ball, and students could choose an activity to participate in. There was less tattling, gossiping, and fighting, and more activity, which made recess much more bearable. This alleviated the habit of the teachers' asking to borrow equipment from the physical education teacher.

ALL CREATURES GREAT, SMALL, . . . AND UGLY

Run for your lives!

"IT'S A PLANE . . . NO, IT'S A . . . " SPLAT

"Hey, look up there!" shouts an excited student. "Wow, cool!" shouts another. "It's just a plane," says a student incorrectly just before being pelted by the object in the sky—not a plane, but a bird. Yes, a bird that had just used his head as a toilet.

I'm surprised that we don't get "dumped on" even more. If you think about how many times birds have flown above you, compared to the number of times you actually have been targeted by a bird that relieves itself, it's amazing. Even at beaches the birds, seagulls, and flying creatures really could do a number on us, but the occurrences are rare.

Obstacle

What do you do when a student gets struck by bird droppings?

Common Mistakes

- Saying, "Ooh, gross."
- Not letting students clean the bird droppings off.

Solutions

- Tell the students the theory that if a bird goes on someone, then that person has been spotted for good luck.
- Smile and say, "Now how would those birds like it if we did that to them?" and send the student in for a cleanup.

Tips

- When it happens, don't allow the other students to make the one who got dumped on feel any worse by their laughing.
- Explain to the group and the student about what it was like when you first "got hit."

Real-Life Story

When John was running the mile he took a hit from our friendly birds in the sky. He was a fast first-grade runner. He thought to himself,

What was that? Then he wondered why the bird did this to him. He had never had this happen before, so why now? Then he figured out why it happened: "Birds normally try to go to the bathroom in open areas to avoid people. But I was running so fast that the bird didn't know I could run into that spot as fast as I did! And that is when the accident happened."

THE WILD, FROM WASPS TO WORMS

You're in the middle of giving directions in a huddle and suddenly the intense listening to your explanation has been disrupted by a student who has jumped up and away from the group. You are thinking, *What in the world is this student doing?* Of course, now all the attention has diverted from you to this student who is swatting and flailing his arms about and screaming. This triggers the other students to let loose and start to flee the scene. They scatter about the field, some screaming, some laughing. All this chaos occurred because a bee flew through your huddle on the way to finding a flower or something to eat.

In another instance, you are demonstrating a catching technique and all eyes should be focused on you. You look at your students and realize that six of them are staring at another girl's arm. So you stop and wait for their attention—but, nothing. These students have discovered how exciting a ladybug can be: "Ooh, look, it's red. Ooh, it's got spots. If you count the spots, it tells you how old it is. Wow, look at its wings."

Some students enjoy anything that flies or squirms, even if it's a worm. Yes, worms have been more exciting than playing a game with footballs or basketballs for some, but it's the shock factor that gets the other students intrigued enough to tune into the squirmy worm that Billy has yanked up from the dirt, instead of focusing on the teacher. Even flies can divert students' attention from the most exciting lessons. Horseflies and deerflies that bite are far more attention getting than watching a swim instructor do his best tricks. It's truly amazing!

Obstacle

How do you handle the distractions and disruptions from nature?

Common Mistakes 🕐

- Getting angry.
- Trying to compete against a creature of nature.
- Ignoring the distraction.

Solutions ✍

- Accept the fact that you will encounter distractions from nature, because your class is held in nature.
- Use a teachable moment to quickly discuss the distraction in a positive manner, and then return to the lesson.
- Discuss the issue of bees, flies, insects, and worms at the beginning of the year. Tell the students the following:

   "You can never outrun a fly, so don't run around trying to get away. Flies are faster than us running. Bees, wasps, hornets, and dragonflies are just as fast."

   "If the bee or fly lands on you, flick it away."

   "If you run it will chase you. The odds are that it will not harm you, but if it does, don't worry, we can take care of you."

- Discuss allergic reactions to stings. The students should let the nurse and all teachers know if they are allergic to something.
- Let the students know that they should leave nature alone: "Look, but don't touch."

Tip 🏃

Take a deep breath, discuss the issue, and reason with the students. Focus on how senseless it is to panic, because panicking is a waste of energy and works you up for nothing. This will help to calm them down and make sense to them.

Real-Life Story 📖

The students in class would get all worked up about the biting flies. So the instructor did a comparison. She said, "OK, watch this. I will stand still and knock the fly off if it lands on me, and Josh will freak out, run around, scream, disrupt everything, and still not get away from the fly." After she calmly avoided the fly by acting cool, Josh hadn't lost the fly and was still looking around excitedly. So she said to the students, "See, if you calmly react to these nuisances they will be more likely to leave you alone. And, we won't lose our PE time!"

HIS BARK IS BIG … AND HE BITES!

"Yikes! There's a dog on the field, there's a dog on the field!" a student screams to you. "Hey, there's a dog on the field!" Naturally, other students begin to scream, some "bark," while others are encouraging the dog to come over to the class. Then, there's always someone who thinks she knows whose dog it is.

Yes, your lesson has been disrupted. But for how long must you endure this dog show? Some dogs are huge, yet they are gentle and mind their own business. Some dogs are small, yet feisty and aggressive. There are the overbearing, loud, hard-to-ignore barks, and some dogs won't even bark at all.

"His bark is bigger than his bite" is the commonly heard expression. But do we really know that? Can we take that chance with 30 students under our supervision? Can we assume that all German shepherds are attack dogs, and all poodles are lap dogs that won't attack? And, how long is this dog going to linger around the area? Because, as long as the dog lingers, the students are going to be distracted. You need to decide if the class should ignore the dog or leave the area, whether students should run away, and if you need to call animal control.

Obstacle

What do you do when dogs interrupt your lesson?

Common Mistakes

- Allowing the students to pet the dog.
- Not having a well-prepared plan that the students know about before the crisis arises.
- Panicking!
- Permitting the dog to run the show.

Solutions

- Discuss the issue of dogs when you discuss "safety in nature's environment," at the opening of the school year.
- Here are some safety ideas:

    Tell students that yes, all dogs have the potential to bite, so they shouldn't pet or call a dog over during class.

If a dog attacks, it will likely jump for the head and face, so tell students that if a stray dog comes up to them, they should fall to the floor and protect their face and head with their hands and arms.

Suggest that they do not run, because the dog will catch them. Dogs are good sprinters.

Advise them not to try to catch the dog.

- Unless it is a dog that you, the teacher, personally know of, you will need to call animal control. This is the best thing for the dog and the public. This way the dog is safe from harm from other animals, other people, and, especially, cars!

- Do not panic! If you are petrified, the students will be doubly scared. Just follow your above rules, and move inside.

Tips

- Keep your fields as enclosed as possible.
- Use the teachable moment to discuss dogs, potential problems with not caring for one's pet, and problems with others not caring for theirs. Tell students that at the animal shelter, the dogs stay in a little area until their owners come to claim them. They are given water and food. The owner will have to pay a small fee. That fee, though, is worth it to make sure that the dog is not run over, hurt, or stolen!

Real-Life Story

The fields at Holland Elementary are not enclosed very well. They back up to people's houses and cul-de-sacs. At least once a month there is a "dog threat" on the fields. Sometimes it's a cute little Pekingese, and sometimes it's a Rottweiler. One day, one of the physical education teachers, Ms. Ewell, started screaming, panic-stricken, to another teacher: "Ms. Somers. Ms. Somers! Ms. Somers!" Ms. Somers wondered what could be wrong with Ms. Ewell. "Look at the dog!" Ms. Ewell cried. She was running around and screaming, yelling at the students to get away from her and not hide behind her. It was obvious to everyone that Ms. Ewell was so scared for her own life that the students were secondary. Finally, Ms. Ewell calmed down, with some help from Ms. Somers, and her group sat in a circle ready to protect themselves. The dog was distracted for a while and animal control took care of the rest.

PLAYING POSSUM

You've heard the expression, "He's playing possum." Someone or something is playing dead by not moving. But how often do you ever really see a possum? And what's the likelihood that one will bother you during physical education?

The students spotted a small "dog" moving slowly in the grass during physical education class. "Oh, I want to go see it!" they pleaded. Ms. Baur kept looking at the animal, puzzled as to what it was. She could tell that it wasn't a dog. But what was it? She wouldn't allow her students to investigate, for who knew what it might turn out to be. Wow, it was a possum! In the middle of the day, in a wide-open field. How often does that occur?

The possum may not appear very often, but other unusual creatures might.

Obstacle

What do you do when a possum or rodent has come to visit, and it is not frightened off?

Common Mistakes

- Becoming too curious and endangering yourself and your students.
- Panicking in front of students.
- Letting the possum ruin your class.

Solutions

- Explain what the animal is.
- Explain the phrase "playing possum": when an animal is scared, it pretends to be dead, so the other animals or people will leave it alone.
- Move away from the animal.
- Call animal control if you feel that it is sick or dangerous to you and the public.
- Keep the class on task. Don't allow the distraction to continue. Redirect the students' attention to the lesson.

Tips 𝕚

- Create a game of "possum tag"—it would be fun and a teachable-moment activity:

    Object of the game: to avoid having to "play possum" by steering clear of danger—the tagger.

    How to play: Five taggers are chosen, and the rest try to avoid being tagged. If they do get tagged, they "play possum" at that point, until someone "unfreezes" them.

- Remember rabies!
- Don't try to be a hero.

Real-Life Story 🖺

While playing a throwing activity, a student saw a small "dog" when he was getting his rag ball. He yelled to everyone to look at the little dog. Of course, they all stopped and looked. Once they got back on task, the physical education teacher realized that it wasn't a dog at all: it was a possum! She wondered what in the world a possum was doing in the middle of the day in the middle of the grassy field, and why it wasn't moving, or running away from the group. Once class was over, and the students left, the teacher went back out to investigate. She thought that it must be dead, or sick, to be in the wide-open field during the day. So she put a cone over it so that an animal-control person could take care of it. She called animal control, and someone arrived about 20 minutes later. She took the animal-control person out to the scene, where he slowly lifted up the cone to uncover the possum. But it turns out that the possum truly had been "playing possum": while the class was inside, the possum had moved out from under the cone and escaped!

And that's what "playing possum" is really about—you wait until the coast is clear, and you make your getaway. Unfortunately, this possum hadn't left the school; it found its way to a food source. There had been a fall dance, with bales of hay and corn still left outside from the weekend. The possum was in search of the corn. After the possum was caught, everyone thought the excitement was over. But like the saying goes, "Where there's one, there's another," the next morning, another possum was found in the boys' restroom. The before-school recreation program had been leaving the doors open, right by the food source. Finally, the physical education teachers, also known as the "commonsense police," convinced the principal to have the corn and hay removed immediately. The possums never came to visit again.

DEAD BIRD ON THE FIELD

Josh was dribbling around the boundaries set up for the activity when he lost control of the soccer ball. He scurried over to retrieve it and screamed out, "Hey, there's a dead bird!" Naturally, the other students said, "Ooh, where? Yuck!" The physical education teacher stopped the class and said, "Boys and girls, there is a dead bird under the tree, but it is way out of our area, so you shouldn't need to get near it if you dribble with control, and especially if you try to avoid the area." So, on went the class, dribbling around the boundaries.

Covered with mud, Josh then came up to the teacher and said, "I fell in the mud." There was no mud around the boundaries. So how did he get muddy? "Where did you fall, Josh?" the teacher asked. He pointed to the area where the bird was. "What were you doing over there?" she asked. "The bird is over there, so you went there on purpose, didn't you?" The teacher sent him inside to clean up. When Josh got back to dribbling, he again slipped and fell in the mud. This was unbelievable! The boy was so intrigued by the dead bird that he lost control and all common sense.

Obstacle

What do you do with dead animals on your playing field?

Common Mistakes

- Not checking the grounds thoroughly before your lesson.
- Expecting kids to be able to ignore such an attraction.

Solutions

- Inspect your area when setting up.
- Remove any dead animal with a stick or gloves, if you are able. If you can stomach it, move it.
- If it needs to be removed and you can't do it, or it is large, call animal control.
- Use common sense: if it's in your area, and the kids are going to be bothered by it, move your lesson to a different area until the problem can be solved.

Tips

- Use the teachable moment to discuss sanitation and the dangers of animal remains:

  They smell.

  They attract scavengers.

  They have diseases that could be transmitted to you.

- If you always check your area, there should not be any surprise dead animals that the students can stare at.

Real-Life Story

The previous anecdote about Josh is true. The fascination with something dead is irresistible to some people. Josh would risk anything—his behavior, disrespect for the instructor's directions, his clothes—not just once, but twice. Where most people would be trying not to look on purpose, some can't help themselves.

BIRD IN THE GYM

Sometimes you just need some fresh air—especially physical education people! We love the real air, and most of us get "stir-crazy" if we can't get outside for a long period of time. When you get confined to your gym because of weather, sometimes you just have to keep the doors open for some genuine, unrecycled air to flow through the sweatbox.

With our doors wide open, we also unintentionally invite guests to check us out: guests such as dogs and cats and even birds. Yes, chirping and all, birds may come in and fly around the gym, swooping and floating above the students and lights.

Obstacle

How do we deal with distractions that we accidentally invite?

Common Mistakes

- Getting angry about a situation that happened accidentally.
- Canceling your lesson.
- Causing widespread panic.

Solutions

- Laugh about the winged guest.
- Discuss with the students when they first get into the gym that there is indeed a bird flying around—in order to get it out of their system.
- Let them look at the bird and talk about it for a minute.
- Organize a game around the bird in the gym. Here's how to play "free the bird": Eight "birds" are designated to fly around a square boundary (the gym). The other students form the square. The object is for the birds to escape from the square without being tagged. If they escape, they join the square.

Tips

- Allow students to watch the bird in the gym. Prohibiting them from this only will result in their sneaking peeks when you're not looking.
- Do a bird movement lesson—flying, swooping, fleeing, flittering, floating, perching, and landing.

Real-Life Story 📖

A bird flew into the gym and hung out around the ceiling for about half the day. The students loved creating methods to help the bird escape:

- Putting some bread near the door.
- Standing by the door and chirping.
- Turning out the lights.
- Playing the music loud.
- Getting a stick and poking the bird out.

The students also came up with the best reasons for why the bird came to visit:

- It must have heard the great music.
- It was probably trying to get out of the rain.
- It was playing hide-and-seek with the other birds.
- It was not sure which way was south so it came to school to learn.

Have fun with these unusual circumstances. They add a little spice to the ordinary.

chapter

7

SNAGS AND INTERRUPTIONS

"WATCH OUT FOR THE—OOPS!—WINDOW"

Your class is throwing back and forth in a catching unit. The object is to throw to a moving target. And the moving target must catch the ball. Suddenly you hear, "Watch out for the ... " *Crash!* " ... window."

Of course, no one intentionally threw the ball to break the window. If someone did, that becomes a discipline issue. But, accidents happen. Especially if you must hold your physical education classes in a classroom or a makeshift gym with windows.

Obstacle

How to avoid hitting a window during physical education.

Common Mistake

Not using your best judgment.

Solutions

- If you have to stay indoors, don't plan throwing activities using any ball other than foam.
- At the beginning of class, discuss staying away from the windows. If someone fails to listen, then that student is unsafe and needs to sit out of the activity until he can be safe.
- Keep the blinds down and closed. This will protect the windows.
- If your class is outside and a ball hits a window, then you should have moved the class farther away from the building. Make sure that all throws are done away from, not toward, the building.

Tip

If the class does break a window, and it was not caused by negligence, you now have a big tool to work with in trying to secure a gym or more space for physical education. With more space, you wouldn't have to worry about breaking a window.

Real-Life Story

For four years Ms. Sullivan had a perfect record with the windows at her school. She had to use the converted old church as the gym. As you can imagine, the old church was full of windows. Suddenly, the record was broken: not during class, but with the physical education helpers trying to move some equipment. A pole flew toward a window and the glass shattered as well as the record. Accidents happen. This was also another step for Ms. Sullivan's school to push for that gym to be built.

WHERE'S THE GYM?

You have just met the principal of the school where you are having a job interview. You are so excited about the opportunity to become a physical education teacher (or about teaching at a new school). Getting a physical education job in many cities is difficult! The principal is talking and giving you a tour of the school. She is asking you some general questions such as what your philosophy of education is and what you would do if you were to teach at this school. You are trying to answer as enthusiastically and intelligently as you can. You get back to her office after you tour the school and sit down across from her desk, ready to be drilled with some more questions. But you have a gigantic question on your mind, and the place you've been dying to see and imagine yourself in has not surfaced.

Where's the gym? Unfortunately, the reason you didn't hear the word "gym" come up is because there is no gym. *What? No gym!* you think. Don't turn and walk away, because there are plenty of ways to run a good physical education program even if you don't have a gym.

Obstacle

> A physical education program without a gym—or, for the old-school types, "gym class" without a gym.

Common Mistakes

- Thinking that you have to have a gym for physical education.
- Not having an open, creative mind.

Solutions

- Do everything you can in the beautiful outdoors! That is the greatest classroom that you could ever have. Unfortunately, it's also not realistic every single day.
- Ask for a meeting room or area. Ask for as much room as possible, yet take what they give you—remember, some physical education teachers have nothing indoors. Have your students meet there for each class.
- Have a flexible relationship with the other teachers so you can use their classrooms when you need to.
- Ask if you could start fund-raisers to build a gym, and work with the principal on that effort.
- Network with other physical education teachers who don't have a gym. On the Web, try PE Central (**www.pecentral.org**) and PE

Links 4U (**www.pelinks4U.org**). Check with other schools and physical education teachers to get ideas.

- Make an area outside your classroom—for example, using the hardtop as a meeting reference place, or the baseball benches to begin and end each class.

- The biggest solution is to be flexible, creative, and positive. The students will love a good program whether they have a gym or not.

Tips

- Make a big deal out of the grounds being your classroom. This will encourage ownership from the students when in that area, and it will help to keep the grounds better maintained.

- Although you have physical education outside most of the time, set your standards for when the class will be staying inside. Have these approved with the principal and distribute them to the teachers in a positive manner, by using a friendly, warm tone. Do this at the beginning of the school year. Here are some standards for having class indoors:

    Too cold = 35 degrees or a windchill of 33

    Too hot = 100 degrees or humidity level of 105

    Rain

    Snow

    Thunder and lightning or threatening weather

Real-Life Story

At Matthew's Elementary School, there was no gym, but there was the potential to design a physical education program that could be great. There was an open area called the "Amen" section of the school that was used as a gathering place after church. The students could meet in there and have tumbling, dance, dribbling, striking, and many other fun physical education activities. It had several windows, but the physical education teacher made sure that she took care of what she had, and she was very careful not to ruin anything.

At White Elementary School, the four backstops of the baseball fields were used to form a makeshift classroom and everything was performed in that area. The distance around the backstops was a quarter-mile, which was great. This made running easy to pace and easy to time. The students at White Elementary became very good runners and would win at every track-and-field meet. They took advantage of what they had; they turned a disadvantage into a winning potential.

IF IT HAPPENED ONCE, IT WILL HAPPEN AGAIN

Thomas is misbehaving, and after you confront him, he quotes a common saying: "It won't happen again," or, "I won't do it again." The very next day, Thomas is play-wrestling again.

A teacher is late picking up her class from physical education. So now you have both that class and the next class, who just entered the gym and are anxiously awaiting the lesson. The teacher arrives five minutes late and is very apologetic. Unfortunately, the following week, she again takes advantage of another free five minutes. She arrives with a different excuse, yet she's still five minutes late.

If it happens once, it probably will happen again.

Obstacle

Problems that repeat themselves.

Common Mistakes

- Stressing over the problems
- Accepting them without confronting the issue.

Solutions

- Address the issue with the person or people who are causing a disturbance.
- Take these suggestions into consideration:

    Talk in a calm voice. Let the other person talk first.

    Ask how the problem or concern can be remedied.

    Document your conversation!

    Be fair yet firm.

    State your reasonable needs.

    See how your plan to compromise and cooperate plays out after your conversation.

- If your talk with a fellow staff member provides no positive results, get a mediator—someone whom you both trust—to listen to the concerns.
- After warnings and effort, take it to the next level:

    If your problem is with a late teacher, discuss it with the principal.

    If your problem is with a misbehaving student, discuss it with a parent.

    If you're dealing with other issues, identify the responsible person who can discuss the issue further.

- After such discussions, you will have to set up your consequences, and follow through. Remember to always consult and get approval from your principal. Possible consequences:

  For a late teacher . . . if he is late picking up his students more than three times, he loses a day of physical education for his students. This is sad for the students, but his negligence is inconveniencing two other teachers and forcing a class of students to lose their physical education time. The principal will give out the discipline and the teacher will have to explain that because of his own negligence, he lost PE class for a day. The other class that missed out gets an extra 10 minutes of class on that day, for the wasted time the students had spent waiting.

  For a misbehaving student . . . if he misbehaves more than three times, he loses a day of physical education because of the disruptions that the other students had to endure. He will not be allowed near the gym, but he may come back once he can behave. The physical education teacher can hand out this discipline sentence.

- If your principal is not supportive, you must let the issue roll off your back. Stick to reason and professionalism.

Tips

- Keep things positive. Only resort to the negative if you have exhausted your positive methods.
- Stay professional. Forgive.

Real-Life Story

A teacher was seven minutes late one day when he came running in and threw an extra jab at a very forgiving physical education teacher: "I know I'm late, and I'm sure it won't be the last time." The physical education teacher was taken aback by the rude comment. There was no apology, no "thank you." Just a feeling of, "I burdened you once, and I will burden you again and not even feel bad about it." The physical education teacher was astonished and kept thinking about it; she couldn't let it go. The next day the same teacher showed up to drop off his students, and the physical education teacher said, "Ooh, could you keep them a second because I need to run to the bathroom." She stayed in there for several minutes and then came back. She said, "I know that took me a while, and I know that won't be the last time." She looked for an expression on the teacher's face and then quickly took the class for physical education. The classroom teacher must have realized, without being confronted, that you do unto others as you would have them do unto you!

JUST WHEN YOU THINK YOU'VE SEEN EVERYTHING . . .

"Oh, my gosh, that is the weirdest thing that has ever happened in my career." This is a statement that may be true for some physical education teachers for a while, but it will be updated before you know it, and before you want it.

Joey was running a quarter-mile, in his usual noncoordinated style. That was just Joey. He was a little goofy but an eager-to-try second-grader. As he was running, the physical education teacher noticed that Joey's PE uniform T-shirt was so long that she could see it below the hem of his shorts. The teacher thought this was what she saw. But she looked closer as Joey jogged to the halfway point, and she noticed the white material slipping lower and lower, below his hemline. She thought that there was no way that a shirt could be tucked into someone's shorts and keep slipping toward the knees. As Joey ran it got worse. You'd think Joey would stop and fix the problem, but it must not have bothered the untidy little Joey. As he jogged, the teacher noticed that there was flesh in between the white material and the hemline of the blue shorts. How could that be?

Puzzled and amazed at Joey's lack of concern about this, the teacher was dying to figure this one out. How in the world he could run with this cloth hanging around his knees was mind-boggling. Finally Joey jogged his last step and joined the forming huddle. The teacher made her way to Joey, who was now looking down at the cloth around his knees. It turned out not to be his shirt, but very loose, baggy, overstretched underwear. The elastic would not stay up around his waist, so as he had run it had slipped down to his knees. When the teacher asked Joey about it, he said that he didn't have any clean underwear, so he was wearing his father's!

Obstacle

Strange happenings that seem to be as strange as they come yet will be outdone by more strange things for you to wonder and think about.

Common Mistake

Thinking that this was the strangest thing that could ever happen to you.

Solution

Always be prepared for a unique, even stranger event to come along and take the title away from the last experience.

Tip

Although the event is not always comfortable at the time it is happening, it provides you with great conversation and memories. You'll be able to laugh and laugh—and astonish others with your experiences.

Real-Life Story

The same teacher had another incident, two years later, at a different school. The students were playing a game of dribbling and tagging. After one of the rounds was over, all the students were back with their teams anxiously awaiting another turn. Somebody shouted, "Oh, yuck, someone's underwear!" *Again with the underwear,* the teacher thought, wondering how underwear could be in the middle of the gym, in the middle of the game. It was a mystery. No one could have run out of their underwear. The teacher looked around and saw that no one was streaking and everyone had their clothes on. Of course, no one would confess to this.

In conclusion, the teacher figured that some student had to go to the bathroom but didn't make it, and he went in his underwear. He didn't want to put the underwear back on, so he stuck it in his pocket. While playing the game, the tagger must have tagged and grabbed a bit, thus pulling the underwear out of the student's pocket. Not only do quality physical education teachers handle teaching, but they also have to do a little private investigative work—"Magnum PE."

chapter 8

WEATHER WOES

RUNNY NOSES

Sniff. Wipe. Sniff. Wipe. That is normal for a physical education teacher to do during the winter. We are outside in the elements for hours, and like a faucet not all the way turned off, the nose just drips because of the cold.

When a student complains of a runny nose, it normally is due to a cold. A student may think that if her nose is running, she is sick and needs to stay in bed. Some students will ask you for permission to go to the bathroom to fix the drip. Others do the simple, outdoorsy thing: wipe it on their sleeve. It's only water.

Then some students have more than that, such as phlegm. The great thing is that everyone is outside, and they don't need to run into the bathroom. They can spit right there.

Obstacle

Handling the runny-nose syndrome.

Common Mistake

Letting the students go into the building to wipe or blow—if you do, they'll probably play around in the bathroom, miss important parts of your lesson, and repeat the performance whenever they want to escape or be alone.

Solutions

- Keep tissues in your first-aid pouch or clipboard (some clipboards have enough room for 100 bandages, gloves, tissues, and more). These can be for the students as well as for yourself.
- Explain that noses run in cold air. When people are outside, the cold air causes their noses to water, but just in little drips, not a stream. It is not phlegm or other things, just tiny drips that shouldn't worry anyone.
- Tell students they may bring tissues if they have a cold.
- Tell them just to sniff, if it's only from the cold air. If it is not just a drop, but rather a gooey glob, that should be handled with a tissue.

Tips

- Remember, you are not the nurse, and you can't have all the first-aid supplies, but tissues can be stuffed in your first-aid pack.

- Before denying a student a tissue, ask her if she has been out sick. You don't want to be stingy; however, if the students see you giving them out all the time, it will become a nuisance to have to give them out several times a class.

Real-Life Story

Kim went up to Ms. Smith, the physical education teacher, and said she was getting a cold and needed to go to the bathroom to get a tissue. Ms. Smith knew that she was a constant complainer and said, "Let me see." She didn't see anything, so she said, "There's nothing there, and a little drip in people's noses in the winter is normal." Kim thought about it, and then she ran back to participate without further incident. Another student, Cindy, came up to Ms. Smith, covering her mouth with her hand. Cindy didn't say anything, so Ms. Smith thought she was going to throw up. She let her go to the bathroom. Cindy did the same thing the very next day, and Ms. Smith asked, "What do you need?" Cindy pointed to her mouth. This time, Ms. Smith wouldn't allow her to go to the bathroom, because she was suspicious. Finally, realizing that she couldn't use this as an attention getter, Cindy said, "I've got to spit." Realizing that Cindy was using this for attention, Ms. Smith "nipped it in the bud" by telling her to poke her head outside the gym door and spit. This curbed her desire to use that excuse anymore.

BATTLING MOTHER NATURE

You have thoroughly thought out and planned your throwing unit for the year. You have written and recorded your weekly plan along with your daily lesson plans. Each of these plans fits into your yearly physical education program plan. You are organized and ready for the week, unit, and year.

Monday arrives and all goes as planned. Tuesday comes, and so does some rain. On Wednesday, the ground is saturated and you are prevented from going outside. It rains again on Thursday. Friday is a wash, because the grounds look like a lake with ducks floating around the large puddles on your fields.

Four out of five days were lost in your throwing unit. Your ideas are all washed away. You think, "How in the world will I make this up and not ruin my yearly plan?"

What's even harder to make up is when the weather is good for part of the day and rotten for the other part. So, half the classes on a Monday get the throwing lesson, while the other half still need it. Scheduling and planning, now, become a bear.

The schools that have physical education only once or twice a week are the real sufferers. Weather can really dampen the program plans. You could have some classes way ahead of others. This also becomes a setting-up nightmare for the physical education teacher.

Another weather worry is what to do with your students in a spur-of-the-moment change of plans. And you wonder how all the equipment will fare in a downpour when your first consideration is getting the students out of the heavy rain, not getting your equipment.

Obstacle

Weather that ruins your plans and your equipment.

Common Mistake

Getting upset and flustered thinking that you have to change your yearly plan by 8 a.m. the next day.

Solutions

- Certain things in life are out of your control. Don't stress about those things. You must let them occur and take it as it comes. The weather will do what it wants, so let this roll off your back.

- Every once in a while it is fun to have to run in from a rain shower and play a makeshift game that the students can participate in without much setup. Organize games that the students know. Have your quick-change bag of tricks handy. (See the "Tips" section for ideas.)

- Students understand an emergency change of plans better than you think. Give them credit and keep them on your side. Once you all are inside, tell them that everyone has to work together in this emergency change of plans. They will enjoy working together with you in such a crisis.

- Work into your yearly plan some unexpected weather day plans. Allot one or two days for makeups and catch-ups. This way when you do lose a day, your whole unit plan isn't shot.

- Have two units in mind at all times: one inside and one outside. If you are outside throwing and get rained out, go into your dance unit for a day. Have your dance lesson plans prepared at the beginning of the year. Keep them accessible and turn to them when needed. Plan your yearly schedule and keep track of which part of your dance unit you've covered. This way you don't have any totally lost days!

- The equipment will have to suffer out in the rain for one class period. Then, when the next classroom teacher arrives to drop off her class, ask if she would mind waiting while you run outside to bring in your equipment, which could get ruined by the rain. The teacher will understand a unique situation like this. Make sure you thank her when you return and take the class.

Tips

- Control what you can, and don't stress about the rest!

- Have a fun weather-disruption game handy. "Four Corners" takes no equipment and keeps everyone moving: The students move about, in various ways that you suggest, until the caller shouts a type of weather. Whatever the caller shouts, the students must do to find a corner in which to hide. The object of the game is to see how lucky a player can get, trying to avoid being in the corner that the caller will say, after he has called the type of weather and a corner number. If a player is in a corner that is not called, she is winning. If she is in the corner that the caller called, she is out, and she must go to the middle and perform the designated exercise that the caller suggests. Here are types of weather movements:

Rain = crawl to corner behind you

Snow = roll to corner in front of you

Wind = leap to corner across from you

Heat = crab walk to nearest corner

Real-Life Story 📖

During a physical education lesson, the clouds started to darken and thicken. As the students looked up, one of them stated, "I hope we get to go in because I love that Four Corners weather game!"

RAINY DAYS AND MONDAYS

Ruined plans and equipment are only part of the problem when Mother Nature gets angry. You've heard the lyric, "Rainy days and Mondays always get me down," from the Carpenters. Well, even the most positive person can start to feel a little "down in the dumps" when the rain starts to interfere with her scheduled plans. Depending on the field conditions, a one-day rain event could mean several days of swamplands or lakefront gym property. A multiday rain event could mean a jail sentence for those who feel trapped with 130 stir-crazy students in the gym at once: "Free me!"

Obstacle

Surviving the many uncontrollable circumstances that excess rain brings:

- Ruined lesson plans
- No fresh air
- Being stuck inside four walls all day—a physical education teacher's nightmare
- No sunlight
- Stir-crazy students
- Too many students in the gym at one time—many schools have more than one class and more than one physical education teacher in the gym at the same time
- Gloom

Common Mistakes

- Letting the rain get you down.
- Not planning for a rainy-day activity before it occurs.
- Not enjoying the challenge of making a quick, successful change in plans.

Solutions

- Make a rainy-day plan to cover skills that can be done inside. Make this plan at the beginning of the school year. Then keep track of what skills have been and need to be covered.
- Have a special "rainy-day activity" that the students love that is only done on rainy days.

- Treat yourself on these days. Have a chocolate treat in between classes, or order out for lunch.

- Allow your rainy day to be your "catch-up" day. Create an activity that will permit you to catch up students who need extra time, for absences, or for those who just need your special attention placed on them. The activities should be less teacher-directed to allow you more freedom. An activity that the students can do without constant feedback from the teacher allows you more time to help individual students while the majority continue with their activity.

- Work out intensely during your exercise portion of class to release the tension. Work out before going to work on a rainy day.

- Allow for these days in your schedule.

Tips

- Play special rainy-day music, such as Jimmy Buffett, to take everyone's mind off the dreary rain and onto beautiful beach scenes.

- Make the activities that you plan for rainy days so exciting that the kids don't mind being stuck inside. My students love when they get to stay in the gym, so they cheer when it is raining. During the school day, if it's raining, the students try to sneak down to the gym to see what fun rainy-day activity is taking place.

- Try this fun rainy-day-centers activity—a good workout!—with four to six students in a group, rotating every three to four minutes:

  Raincoat relay race—students put a coat on, do a locomotor activity, then pass it on to the next team member.

  Swing over the swamp—they swing from the climbing rope to a safe, dry spot.

  Jump the puddles—they jump over Hula Hoops.

  Flee the flood—in this tagging activity, the flood is "it" and the others run from the flood.

  Dodge the rain—two groups are on either side of the rope or net, set at least five feet tall, and the students must throw yarn balls or soft, light Nerf balls over the net to attempt to land the "raindrop" on someone, while the other group must let it land on the floor before someone can touch the rain/ball.

Hydroplaning—one student sits on a carpet square while the other pulls him around by a rope.

Real-Life Story

During rainy days I like to play Jimmy Buffett, or the "beachy" songs, throughout the activities. It takes my mind off of the dreariness and into the pleasing atmosphere of the sun, the beach, relaxing, playing, swimming, and enjoying myself. It's my little "Gym-aritaville."

FLUFFY, POOFY, AND SCARY

I get worried about some quirky things that most people wouldn't waste a second thinking about. Kids, I've noticed, have issues and worries that I wouldn't have even considered.

Jimmy, a first-grader, was hesitant to go outside one day. He went out with the group, reluctantly, but he wouldn't do anything except stand right next to the teacher's leg, like a small child afraid to leave his mommy or daddy. The next day, Jimmy's father showed up for physical education class.

These thoughts went through the teacher's mind:

- *Why is he here?*
- *What did I do wrong?*
- *The child couldn't be frightened of me—I'm not scary or intimidating.*
- *I didn't say anything that would upset anyone.*
- *I've got to ask him why he is visiting.*

Be prepared for the answers and reasons you get, because they are not always predictable. In fact, some will be incredibly bizarre.

Are you ready for this one? It turned out that Jimmy was afraid of clouds. Yes, white, fleecy, fluffy, dark, thick, rolling clouds. So, did that mean that he should stay inside every time the clouds were in the sky? How often do you have a day when there is not a cloud in the sky?

Obstacle

What issues, concerns, illnesses, disorders, and problems do you take seriously, and what do you let roll?

Common Mistakes

- Being too lenient with students' woes. If you didn't push some students, especially first-graders, they wouldn't do much of anything. You have to nip some problems "in the bud" and encourage students to perform the tasks that you have planned for them.

- Not being concerned with students' issues. If you don't let a student explain his situation, he might view physical education, you, and even the school with some negative feelings.

Solutions

- Review student issues and medical concerns with the school nurse or the principal. (Most medical issues you will notice at this time. The odd ones you'll have to encounter as they pop up.)

- When something odd occurs, listen. Listen to the dilemma, then ask questions. Listen to what the student, the parent, the nurse, the principal, a counselor, and the classroom teacher have to say.

- Once you are informed, try to allow that student to participate as if there were nothing preventing him from performing as the other students do. Encourage him a little extra to get in there and do his best.

- If a student can't function well in a situation, encourage her to participate and try to overcome her obstacles—and not let them overcome her.

Tips

- Be prepared for some unique situations.
- When you think you've heard everything, you can bet that something will come along to blow away your complacency.

Real-Life Story

Chelsea, a first-grader, was so cute and sweet. Suddenly, one day, she refused to move for the physical education teacher. She didn't line up when the teacher asked her to. Finally, a student just grabbed her hand and walked her to the gym. The next day she was laughing and participating in the activity with no problems, but then, when the other students were walking toward the gym to leave, Chelsea was standing on the hardtop crying her eyes out, with her hands up in the air and shoulders shrugged. She wouldn't budge. After speaking to the appropriate people, the teacher was astonished but educated about a new disorder or phobia that someone could have. Chelsea's problem will seem incomprehensible to many; however, it is true. Chelsea was afraid of leaving the ground. She didn't want to pick up her feet, because her phobia caused her to fear being off the ground. So if she didn't move, she was safe.

"MY FUTURE'S SO BRIGHT"

You will need to wear sunglasses outdoors, no doubt about it. You are outside for six hours a day. You have to protect those wonderful eyes that help you see the beauty in the world. If you don't wear sunglasses, you will cause yourself agitation and potential eye problems and you could miss something that's going on because of the sun's blinding rays. Sure, you look cool in those shades! But that's not why you're going to be wearing them.

Looking cool is definitely a desire most young people have. Don't be surprised when you see a student showing up to class with his sunglasses on: yes, the first-grader as well as the twelfth-grader. You do it, so why can't they?

That student with those fake Oakleys thinks he is looking very cool. That first-grader just loves her big Mickey Mouse glasses. If you're distracted, you can bet the students wearing them and their classmates are distracted, too.

Obstacle

Students wearing sunglasses and hats that distract themselves and others.

Common Mistakes

- Being hypocritical—telling students that they may not wear those "cool shades" during your class just because it doesn't seem right.
- Not discussing this at the beginning of the school year.

Solutions

- Discuss the use of protective gear, such as hats and sunglasses, and explain why the students should wear them.
- Set the rules regarding sunglasses and hats:

    Sunglasses may be worn only over the eyes, not on the head for fashion. Some students think it is cool to wear the glasses on the head, not intending to use them to protect the eyes.

    Hats may be worn only outside of the building. If your school allows hats in the building, don't worry.

    Everyone should take off sunglasses and hats upon entering the gym.

Tip

> At the beginning of the school year, take some time for a teachable moment about how to protect oneself from the sun. Be sure to discuss sunglasses, hats, wearing light clothing, and using sunblock or sunscreen.

Real-Life Story

A boy who wanted to be cool wore sunglasses to physical education class. His purpose was not to help himself see in the sun's bright rays, but to get attention and look good. The reason the teacher knew this was because he wore them on top of his head during the whole class. This was discussed and remedied, so that everyone understood that it's OK for students to look cool while trying to protect themselves—they shouldn't, however, just try to use physical education as the time to show off their outdoor gear.

"I CAN'T FEEL MY TOES"

"Hey, there goes my breath," the line leader says as he walks out the gym doors, leading the class into the raw winter weather that awaits. As the students follow, you hear, "Ooh, it's cold," from every other student who crosses that doorway. You already know it's cold because you have to be out in it for six shivering hours.

Three layers on your upper body, thick-lined shell pants, gloves, earmuffs, a hat, and a warm, thick coat are helping you cope with the winter chill. You aren't too cold, but it's bitter enough to be uncomfortable.

The weather forecast is available for everyone to see on television, hear on the radio, or read about in the newspaper. However, you have children who show up to physical education class with a light windbreaker jacket and complain the entire time. You have to wonder what their parents are thinking about when they send their little ones off to school like this.

The show must go on. With five physical education teachers sharing the gym, some groups have to go outside during the cold season. You do whatever you can to keep their minds focused on the objective and the task you've planned. You think they'll all make it through the class even if their noses are red, their cheeks are rosy, and their lips are shivering. But when a well-behaved, noncomplaining student taps you on the arm and looks pitifully up at you and says, "I can't feel my toes," then it's time to go in.

Sometimes we have to give in to the weather, and we always have to listen to our bodies. When a good student sincerely advises you of the numbness in her extremities, it's time to give in to the nasty wintry weather and change your plans.

Obstacles

- Freezing temperatures that make your lessons miserable and the students miserable too.
- Students who come to school unprepared for the weather conditions.
- Keeping yourself warm for six hours.

Common Mistakes

- Trying to be too tough.
- Trying to get kids to stop complaining about the temperature by telling them something like, "When I was in school, we ran the mile run in the snow and still scored the presidential score, wearing snow boots and shoveling our way through the track."
- Not remembering that safety is always first!
- Forcing the students to participate while uncomfortable.

Solutions

- Set a comfortable standard:

    Do not go out if temperatures are below 35 degrees.

    Do not go out if the windchill is below freezing.
- If you are uncomfortable, the students probably will be too.
- Realize that students will not benefit from the lesson if they can't concentrate or feel their fingers or toes.
- Change activities in the wintry months, so that you spare yourself and your students misery.

Tips

- Imagine how you would feel in the students' position.
- If you are sliding on ice in the field, then it's too cold to be outside.
- If the students huddle together and won't participate in their favorite warm-up, then it's too cold.
- If you have to wear a ski mask, then don't go out.
- Plan the following skills during the winter months:

    Educational gymnastics

    Rhythmic movements

    Dance

    Dribbling

    Circuit training/body awareness/fitness

    Basketball, throwing, and catching (March Madness)

All of the above have been tried, tested, and approved, even with groups of 150 in a small gym (the size of a basketball court, with no space for bleachers).

Real-Life Story 📖

The students failed to get involved in their favorite activity and huddled together as if to save each other from the brutally cold wind. Mr. McLemore yelled at the students to stop crying and get to work. "What's wrong with you? We can't always have 80-degree days, you know!" he stated with great frustration. He was furious that the students were defying him and not participating. Mr. McLemore finally realized that no one was benefiting from the lesson.

Even if students respect you, they have basic needs and instincts. Mr. McLemore also realized that you can't force things—sometimes you have to be even more flexible than you think you already are. And were those students pleased with him when they retreated and went inside!

"IT'S TOO HOT!"

Every physical education teacher that I know, and every student that I know, looks forward to summer. The weather is good in the summer for doing activities outside, such as swimming, surfing, softball, baseball, T-ball, volleyball, tennis, and just about every other sport!

In my area of the country, the weather finally breaks around March. It starts to get nicer, and hotter. Now those lucky people who have 70 degrees all year long wouldn't quite know the feeling, but imagine December, January, and February staying below 40 degrees. When you start to see and feel the temperature rise, it gives you a great feeling of being "free"—free from wearing all that heavy gear to stay warm, free from shivering, and free to start new skills and units that the cold weather kept you from doing.

Sometimes the students who dreaded the cold, and complained about it, then cry, "It's too hot!" in the warm months. After all that cold weather, freezing their fingers as they threw the ball, they now complain about being hot. They are moping around instead of being the vibrant group you've seen before. You feel like you just can't win. What's the answer? You keep them inside when it's too cold, so do you keep them inside when it's too hot? And what's too hot?

Obstacle

What do you do when the students say, "It's too hot"?

Common Mistakes

- Caving in to their complaints.
- Not being concerned about the heat.
- Creating lessons that are too vigorous for the heat.

Solutions

- Always check the forecast the night before and in the morning, for the temperature and the heat index for that day.
- At the beginning of the school year, discuss weather issues with your students:

Tell them that you never would ask them to do something that you wouldn't do yourself, in the same conditions. (If you live by this rule, it makes it easier.)

Tell them that you never would endanger them by forcing them into dangerous weather conditions.

Tell them that safety is always number one!

Let them know that the class will not go outside if the temperature is above a certain number or if the heat index is above a certain point. So they shouldn't complain about the heat because it has been discussed already.

- To cover yourself, discuss safe conditions with your supervisor and principal, and agree on a rule for when you should bring a class inside.

- When the temperature is above 90 degrees, plan activities that do not require much physical exertion.

Tips

- Do not do physical fitness testing in temperatures or heat indexes that are above 90 degrees.
- Plan activities with minimal running.
- If you want students to do a lap, wait until the end of the lesson so that they will give you 100 percent during the lesson.
- Some ideas for hot-weather days:

  Volleying and volleyball

  Softball

  Swimming (for those lucky enough to have a pool!)

  Badminton and striking

  Croquet and striking

  Golfing and striking

  Four-square

  Frisbee throwing

  Bowling and rolling

  Horseshoes and throwing

  Ring toss and throwing

Real-Life Story

As soon as the weather was above 70 degrees and the students would break a sweat, someone would say, "I am hot." This was the perfect time for me to say, "Remember our rule about weather." As soon as I'd state this, the students would realize what they were doing and stop complaining.

"THERE GO ALL THE BALLS"

While you are giving instructions to your rowdy, windblown fifth-graders, two students attempt to blurt out while you are speaking. You have warned them about being disrespectful and not to interrupt during the time you are giving instructions. Again, the students attempt to overthrow your rule on blurting out. You quickly shush them. Then, not being able to restrain himself, a very polite student blurts out, "Excuse me, but there go all the balls down the street." You look, and sure enough, at 20 miles per hour gust speed, the balls are rolling down the road.

Obstacle

Windy days that cause havoc with your equipment and lessons.

Common Mistakes

- Not adjusting your lesson to fit the weather circumstances.
- Ignoring the weather circumstances.
- Fixing your hair on a windy day.

Solutions

- Be flexible! Your job depends on the weather to do certain things for you. You need the sun and rain to provide grass for you to have a field. You also will have to put up with the weather when it involves wind. As a physical education teacher, be prepared to change plans.
- Always have a backup plan! You never know what will happen from day to day.
- Don't plan volleyball, volleying, badminton, or tennis in the spring. The wind is in its prime during March, April, and May.
- Use equipment that can hold up in the wind! No birdies, beach balls, foam balls, Wiffle balls, or light equipment.
- Keep your equipment in a safe, enclosed cart or bag that cannot be blown around.
- Watch the weather the night before and in the morning before you go to work.

- Wear more, or bring clothes, jackets, and protective gear to shield you from the elements.
- Warn the students of the wind condition. Get this out in the open right away, so that you can move on with your lesson.

Tips

- Always have a hat handy—it will help keep your hair from flying all over the place at work. If you are a man, however, check with your principal to make sure that it's not disrespectful to wear a hat in your building or for work. You also could wear a cap with your school's logo on it.
- The students may get a little out of control; the wind seems to blow silliness into their brains.
- Ears are sensitive. Protect yours by wearing a wrap, a hood, or earmuffs.
- The temperature may be 60 degrees, but if there is a windchill of 40 degrees, it can turn a nice, gentle day into a cold, chilly, even miserable day because of the wind.
- Use examples to show how windy the day will be and make the students laugh. Then it's out of their system, and you and they can get on with the class objective.

Real-Life Story

The equipment for the day required two cage balls. Everyone loves a cage ball! After lunch, the teacher went out with his class to begin the lesson, when he discovered that one cage ball was missing. He was so angry. While he was telling the students how mad he was that someone would steal the school's ball, a student yelled out, "Hey, there's our ball!" The ball was rolling down the street in the adjacent neighborhood. The embarrassed teacher now switched the blame to himself, and he apologized for accusing someone of stealing.

chapter
9

OUTSIDE ANNOYANCES

HEARING OVER THE HONKING

"Get a partner, and volley as high into the sky as you can. Then, take the ball and—vvvrooom, honk, honk." This is what the students hear as they are carefully listening and awaiting the directions for an activity from their teacher. They could fill in the blanks: "Oh, she must have said, 'Run around and throw it at people,'" or, "Maybe she said, 'Spike it at your partner as hard as you can.'"

Of course, the teacher didn't say these things, but when something uncontrollable such as traffic and honking drown her voice out, it's as if she has given the class a free pass to "go wild" and not listen. The car is disrespecting her, and the students seem to think it's OK to talk to others and fidget when a vehicle interrupts their teacher's instructions.

If you teach where there is a lot of traffic, you are going to hear lots of honks. It will be really annoying if you don't create a plan for dealing with it. And you need to create a plan for ignoring the steady car noise.

Obstacle

> How do you handle the distracting noises that are unavoidable when you are outside, such as car engines and honking?

Common Mistakes

- Letting the cars and honking get on your nerves.
- Allowing the uncontrollable distractions to control your class.

Solutions

- When loud cars drown you out, do the following:

    Pretend you are saying something by mouthing words, and once the car noise has passed, ask your students what they think you were saying.

    Have the students do an action during the distraction (e.g., stretching or an exercise).

- If the roar is constant, you must let it roll off your back. You cannot stop the traffic, so work with your circumstances and ignore the noise.

Tips

- Create an activity to do when truckers honk:

    Sing a song.

    Wave.

- Move your class as far away from the road as you can.
- Project your voice. Dig deep. Don't scream over the cars.
- If it is annoying enough to you, then get a new job at another school. You'll never stop the traffic.

Real-Life Story

Truckers would honk on a regular basis during the day. The students got used to this and would look, wave, and continue with their activity. As an assessment and interlinking activity, the students would write letters to their trucker buddies and tell them about the activities and skills that they were working on.

POLICE CARS, FIRE TRUCKS, AND AMBULANCES

When sirens sound and police cars speed past your field of activity, you can bet your students will take notice. That siren is the sound that someone is in trouble, about to get arrested, or hurt. When the students hear the sirens, their curiosity takes over, and they say, "Hey, what's going on?" and speculate about the reasons for the commotion. They buzz about wondering and can't possibly keep throwing the ball if the exciting sirens are blaring. It's like rubberneckers at an accident.

Unfortunately, some schools hear this much more than others. Some students may have rarely heard a siren, but with the proliferation of TV shows about the police and medical professions, most students have an idea of what that siren is racing toward. Whether or not they are familiar with the noise, you can bet they will turn their heads when the siren's wail nears.

Obstacle

What do you do when the sirens blast past your class?

Common Mistake

Getting angry at children when they stop to look.

Solutions

- Acknowledge the sirens.
- Discuss the reason they are here: to help people. The students should not be afraid because the emergency vehicles make people feel better. The police are going after people who are causing trouble or breaking the law, so the kids should have no fear.
- Create a special activity to perform when the sirens blare through a lesson: for example, when sirens are heard, each student stops what he is doing and performs a physical activity (a lap while making the noise of a siren, or jumping jacks and making the noise). This will release the pent-up curiosity and energy that the students have.

Tip

Realize that some students might fret and possibly bolt from your class because they fear that someone's life is in danger, are afraid of loud noises, or have been brought up to run from the noise.

Real-Life Story

During a throwing lesson, an ambulance drove right up to the school. The students instantly dropped what they were doing. They started talking among themselves and guessing what might be wrong. Then they started to get upset about what could be happening. Their curiosity increased as did their worrying. The teacher had to yell in order to get them to huddle up, discuss the issue, and calm down. The students who could continue started to throw, but they kept one eye on the ambulance. The others sat out on their own and eventually joined in once they realized that the ambulance and its crew take care of people in trouble. As students, they need to trust the medical crew; if it's the students' business, they'll find out what happened.

"WHAT'S THAT SMELL?"

"Mmm, I smell food," is a comment that you'll hear from time to time, whether the smell is from your own cafeteria or from a local fast-food restaurant. You'll undoubtedly hear, "I'm hungry," or, "What's for lunch?" from your students. You'll be hungry, too, if you smell food like French fries and fried chicken for a few hours.

Ah, the fresh scent of newly cut grass, or of honeysuckle. It's pleasing to the senses and gives you one more reason to love being outside. No stale classroom air, just fresh outdoor air!

Then, one day, the class will walk out the door and suddenly everyone will be holding their noses and exclaiming about a bad smell. When something outside smells, it usually lasts for a while. Each time workers put mulch down on the playground, you'll have at least a full day of a "manure" odor. Or roofers will use tar when they work on the roof, creating an unpleasant smell that you can't seem to escape.

Obstacle

Keeping students' minds off the smells of the outdoors and on the lesson.

Common Mistake

Getting upset over the students' comments.

Solution

As soon as the students come outside and notice the aroma, whether it's good or bad, make a lighthearted comment or a joke. Once the students have laughed about the odor, bring them into a huddle, discuss the smell, and insist that the class will continue regardless of the smell.

Tips

- Inform the students that you have to be outside dealing with the smell all day long.
- Organize warm-up games that include the smell, such as "smelly tag": Ask the students to try to name the odor or aroma that they smell, such as manure, dog excrement, cow pasture, or dirty diapers. Then ask four students to be "it"—they represent the odors. The others flee from the "smell" in a game of tag.

- If the smell is pleasing, yet still distracting, include that in your lesson:

    Drop the chicken in the fryer (throwing to targets)

    Flip the burgers (striking with paddles and beanbags or balls)

    Make a pizza (throwing and catching Frisbees)

Real-Life Story

At least twice a year, mulch is delivered to the playground for fall areas—and does it stink! So, to play along with the unavoidable circumstances, the students play a "farm" activity and make a joke out of a bad situation instead of staying miserable. Then there are laughs rather than complaints.

chapter
10

FIELD FUN AND FRUSTRATION

"I CAN'T FIND MY FEET"

It's a balmy, beautiful 80 degrees outside. You and your students couldn't wish for a more perfect physical education day! You created the best kicking activity, and you can't wait to treat your students to this lesson. You're envisioning the black-and-white soccer balls being trapped, passed, and kicked from player to player. A keep-away kicking warm-up will be just the trick to get these kids pumped for the lesson.

You step through the gym doors to check out the field and your face drops. Your excitement is shattered. Your plans, spoiled. You can't believe that no one has taken care of this problem.

Not an inch or two or three—but eight inches of grass await you. It's a sea of green beyond that gym door. Stepping into the field of tall grass, you can even feel some blades stretching as high as your thigh. You have called repeatedly about getting the grass cut, yet there's always an excuse for why it hasn't been cut. Of course, none of these excuses is valid to you, but the priorities of the grass cutter and the teacher are two different things. And you still have a physical education class to teach whether the grass is one inch high or eight inches.

Obstacles

- You can't find your feet when you look down because they are covered in grass.
- The balls won't travel when rolled or kicked because the grass stops the momentum.
- The students are itching and scratching a lot!
- The bugs are unbearable.
- When the kids squat down, the grass tickles their rear ends.
- The Bermuda grass and crabgrass trip up the students as they run, unaware of the hidden grass traps.
- During the mile run or a sprint the students appear to be in slow motion because of hurdling the grass.

All of the above indicate the grass may be too high.

Common Mistakes

- Not calling and complaining about the grass.
- Taking it too seriously, and letting it ruin your plans.
- Acting as if nothing is wrong.

Solutions ✍

- Create a clever activity to get you through the situation. A good example is "quick grass," a warm-up activity. The idea of quick grass is similar to quicksand. Divide the class into three groups:

  Taggers (five students)—they run around trying to tag people

  Grass cutters (three students)—they try to "unfreeze" tagged people

  Grass, when "frozen" (the rest of the students)—they run away from taggers; if tagged, they stand still and hope that a grass cutter will "unfreeze" them

  The students run around to try to avoid the taggers. Once the taggers tag them, they get stuck in the extra-long grass and must stand still, because if they move, the grass will pull them down more. The grass cutters will look for the still, tall grass and mow it down ("unfreeze"), and then that student is freed.

- Explain the grass situation to the students and modify the lesson, allowing them to experience the difference the resistance makes. This would interlink well with science.

Tips 🖐

- Have fun with your circumstances—find the bright side.
- Students love unique situations. Make this memorable.
- Warn the students about the potential irritations that grass can deliver, and tell them to be careful to pick up their feet when playing in the grass.
- Be flexible yet cautious.

Real-Life Story 📖

School had just begun, and the landscapers had not yet cut the grass to make the opening of a new school year look inviting as everyone returned to school. The principal had called the landscapers to "get on the ball." The physical education teacher, Ms. Stewart, had called to complain about the tall grass. Their answer was always, "We'll get right on it as soon as we can, but we are really backed up because of the weather." On occasion they would say, "Your day is on Thursdays, so we'll have to wait until Thursday to visit." Each day that went by, either the principal or Ms. Stewart called, trying to get results. Ms. Stewart had to get the students outside—she had 125 kids at a time, so it got cramped and everybody would get antsy when trapped inside.

So, with the proper warning and prior prepping, the students tracked outside to the long, tickling grassy fields. They played some fun "can't find my feet" activities. In one activity they were instructed to find a toe and tap it 10 times first: each student had a partner and stood face to face, holding each other's shoulders, attempting to tap the toe of the partner 10 times before the other person taps it. Another activity was "quick grass," and the students had a great time. Even now, when the grass is an acceptable height, the students will ask if they can play those "can't find my feet" activities.

PLAYING IN THE PASTURE

All of the students are gathered around you in a nice huddle. Suddenly, John looks to the left, and then right, and grabs his nose and squeezes. Tom, who isn't very considerate or conscious of others, blurts out during the instruction: "Ooh, what stinks? I smell poop." So now everybody is looking around, checking the sole of their shoes and moving about.

When you've got a nice, wide-open area like ball fields and school fields, some smart dog walker is definitely going to take advantage of the wide-open space! They don't see kids running about and playing at the moment, so they justify the dog's actions by thinking that this isn't hurting anyone.

There is no poop patrol. You will never be able to stop all the suspects.

Obstacles

- Dog excrement on the field.
- The smell of dog mess during your lesson, and the preoccupation of the students affected by it.
- Getting rid of it.

Common Mistakes

- Ignoring it—it won't go away!
- Not taking action.

Solutions

- First, as you should always do, check the grounds before you set up your equipment!
- You are a grown, mature person. If the mess is in your way, put on your gloves, or get a stick, and move it.
- If a child steps in it, discuss it briefly, and allow that person to wipe the shoe in the grass until it's off.
- Use this as a teachable moment. Discuss the importance of following the courtesy laws and the laws of some states. Tell the students about doing the right thing if their dog—or the dog of someone they know—relieves itself on school property, the ball fields, or anyplace where something could be ruined. Explain what it would be like if they stepped in or sat on it accidentally.

Tips

- The more you stress to your class the importance of encouraging the community to respect the school grounds, the less likely you are to have problems from the carelessness of others.
- When it does happen again, the students will be more concerned about being angry at the community for being disrespectful than they will about laughing at the student who just stepped or sat in the mess.

Real-Life Story

Barbara stepped in a pile of dog mess. She knew she would be laughed at, so she started chasing the other students, who quickly ran from her and screamed. She thought she would share the burden that she had just been given, by threatening to put it on whomever she could catch. The teachable moment came into play. Barbara may have been unfortunate, but should her mess have to be smeared to make others miserable? "Do unto others" can be used often, and it's a great lesson that physical education teachers should emphasize!

BEWARE . . . IT'S THE LAWN-MOWER MAN

Ah, yes, how beautiful it is to see a field or yard that has been groomed and freshly cut! The grass will be better to run, catch, kick, and play in, when it's cut at a good length.

You neatly set up all of your equipment in the morning for your six classes. It takes about 20 minutes to set up, but that's expected. Your orange cones, carpet squares, and red, yellow, and blue balls are aligned just right for your classes to arrive upon a pleasing setup of an exciting activity.

As the students become deeply involved into the throwing and catching game, you see a vehicle barreling through the field, dodging the monkey bars, spinning out in the sand, and heading in a direct path toward you. It can't be anyone else but . . . the "crazy lawn-mower man"! At least, he seems crazy to you. He's trying to mow the same grass on which your class currently is playing a game!

Obstacles

- Do you stop and move, or does he?

- There is noise, noise, and more noise.

Common Mistakes

- You are all set up for your activity, so you assume he should cut the grass around you.

- You assume his time is more important and that you should move for him to get his job done.

- You move out of his way, and he takes a lunch break.

Solutions

- Communicate with the other side and reach a compromise. Talk to the lawn-mowing staff to find out where they will mow first, and work out a deal, so that you both get your job done with the least amount of frustration.

- Get to know your service crew. Once you know each other they are more likely to work with you, not irritate you!

- Find out their schedule, and work out a different lesson on the lawn-mowing day.

Tips 🏃

- Be happy that your grass is going to look much better. Let the change in plans roll off your back.

- Once you are on good terms with the lawn service people, they will want to please you. You wave, you smile, you both do your jobs, and you both make a potentially bad situation a positive experience.

- Get to know the lawn-mowing worker's supervisor so you can discuss the situation with the person who is most likely to make the schedule.

Real-Life Story 📖

7:45 a.m.: The lawn mowers and weed eaters were out in full force. So the physical education teachers set up their equipment where the lawn mowers were not.

8:00 a.m.: The mowers stopped, the workers chatted for 30 minutes, and then they started again.

9:00 a.m.: They drove away, off the school grounds.

11:00 a.m.: They arrived back on the scene. They parked their machines and went to lunch until noon.

12:15 p.m.: They started up again. The teachers still were patiently waiting to move their equipment to a spot where the lawn was cut, so that the lawn-mower men could finish. However, they only had cut for 45 minutes out of four hours. So, the day was shot. Instead of mowing where the students could play, the men were mowing outside of the boundaries of the fields.

1:15 p.m.: Only one class left. The lawn-mower man needed to mow that particular spot where all the students and equipment were. So the teachers moved all the equipment, saying, "Let's just do it, and tomorrow it will be all done."

2:00 p.m.: The classes were finished for the day. Now the lawn-mower man could finish.

2:01 p.m.: The teachers heard the machines cut off. The workers were finished for the day; they would have to return tomorrow.

You can bet that next time the teachers will communicate in advance and find out when the next grass-cutting day is.

THE DAY AFTER

Eight hundred kids running around, playing, screaming, and learning is what you would find at your school fields from 8:00 a.m. to 3:00 p.m. A neighbor can't even walk out of her house without being noticed by the students or a teacher.

Once the teaching day is over, however, and the sun goes down, the place changes its personality altogether. There is not a soul to be found. Or, should I say, there is not a soul to find out what is going on during these dark, private, unpopulated hours.

The school provides a quiet parking lot, steps, things to lean on, protection from the wind, privacy, an interesting apparatus to play on, benches, and freedom from adults, authorities, and others who might not approve of activities that one could do in this environment.

Evidence of this after-school activity can be discovered the morning after a "night of passion" has occurred. You walk out with your class of fifth-graders and there it is: a condom in full view of all the curious students, who look, snicker, giggle, and laugh. The first-graders walk out with you and instead of looking and laughing, one runs over to pick up the long, cream-colored, deflated balloon and says, "Look what I found!"

Obstacle

Condoms and other evidence of sexual conduct on your school grounds.

Common Mistakes

- Allowing the students the opportunity to witness the evidence.
- Allowing the students to pick up and play with this unsightly evidence.

Solutions

- Every single morning, without fail, check your grounds. You never know what you might discover on the fields after a night free from supervision, lights, and surveillance.
- If you continue to have trouble with this, consider getting more lighting or a camera system.
- Ask the police to patrol the area and make their presence known.

Tips

- Bring gloves!
- Carry a trash can or bag with you as you check the grounds.
- If something is overlooked, and a student encounters this type of item, you should use this as a teachable moment. Don't explain "the birds and the bees" to the students, but do explain that anything that is left outside from someone else is to be left alone. Many germs and undesirable things can be on or around these items. Tell them to be safe and don't touch!

Real-Life Story

A class takes an alternate route to the basketball courts. While they walk to their destination, a busy student looks in the direction of a portable classroom and sees something unusual. He runs over and picks up the "pretty balloon" and tries to blow it up. By the time the teacher realizes it is a condom, the awkwardness already has happened.

TRASH OVERFLOW

There are two entrances to your fields. One entrance has a trash can chained to the fence. It's overflowing with Big Gulp cups, soda cans, chip bags, stinky fast-food bags, and beer bottles. Another trash can is chained to the other entrance of the field, and it's overflowing with the same sort of smelly, unsightly garbage. How are you going to get onto the fields? It sure is not a welcoming sight to start your class.

Obstacles

- Ooh, that smell!
- The bees, the wasps, the flies, the birds, and the scavenging kids.
- The eyesore.

Common Mistakes

- You let the garbage "eat" at you, and you obsess about the problems.
- You don't react and the trash remains, the insects increase, and the problem grows.

Solutions

- Call the school's maintenance department and report the situation in a calm yet firm tone. Tell them the following:

    The trash is attracting bees, wasps, hornets, and yellow jackets.

    The insects can injure the students.

    Students could be allergic to insects and not only get worked up but also have a serious attack.

    They could go into anaphylactic shock: a person who is allergic to an insect and has been exposed previously to the source could go into a type of shock brought on by the bite or sting.

    Dogs and cats are hanging around the garbage.

    The trash is terrible to look at.

    The smell is unbearable.

    Ultimately, it is preventing the teacher from teaching and the students from learning.

- Be sure to get your principal and supporters to understand the situation and rally around you.

Tips

- Call early, call late, but don't hesitate to take care of the situation.
- Set up an arrangement for more frequent trash pickups.
- Establish good communication with and feelings toward the maintenance crew. You want them working for and with you, not against you.
- Stay pleasant, yet driven.

Real-Life Story

Hot dog holders with ketchup and mustard were attracting plenty of insects and birds to the trash cans. At night, however, the cute raccoons came for a visit. They dumped over the trash cans and the trash was spread all over the place.

GRAFFITI

"School sucks: Skinheads rule!" is splattered in white and black paint on the brick wall outside of the gym. First you are astonished, then you get mad, and then you've got to take action. It is amazing how skillful these vandals are. Their vandalism is sometimes like a work of art. Then sometimes, it is as disgraceful as the act.

Obstacles

- Graffiti, which will attract the attention of the students.
- Obscenities in plain view of students.

Common Mistakes

- Ignoring it—you can't claim ignorance, you are a professional educator for children.
- Not reporting it—it's vandalism.

Solutions

- First, contact your principal. Let her make the decision about whether to call the police. She also will need to make arrangements to get the graffiti cleaned up as fast as possible.
- Hold your classes in an area where the graffiti will not cause such a distraction.
- Use this as a teachable moment. Tell your class the following:

  Graffiti is defacing someone's property.

  Graffiti on a public school property is defacing government property.

  Police can charge the suspects and it could go on their record.

  The suspects have caused an inconvenience to the class, the school, and the police.

  The suspects have cost some parties money and have cost everyone time and energy.

Tip

Choose an activity to fit the situation. The students will learn many lessons in one—a physical skill, interlinking with spelling, and social awareness:

- "Scribble dribble": The students dribble a ball on the ground attempting to spell out letters to form a word. Each time the ball hits the ground, they should imagine that it is a pen, paintbrush, or paint can marking a spot on the floor and creating part of a letter.
- "Body spelling": The students work as a group while attempting to spell words by shaping their bodies into letters. This can be done on the ground or by standing. An example is "Y M C A."

Real-Life Story

When there was graffiti at Dutch Elementary, the principal was very quick to respond. She had the cleanup team out to work before the first class even noticed the graffiti was there. She discussed the importance of cleaning it up, due to the damage it could cause if students saw it. The cleanup team was sent out immediately, due to her sense of urgency.

POST-PARTY EVIDENCE

Silver Bullets were visible from the threshold of the gym doors. They were scattered throughout the school field, shining as the sun beamed down, making it impossible not to notice them. There were Magnums and Colt 45s and some Budweisers. It was obvious that people had visited the field last night and enjoyed some beer! They probably played a little softball, talked and joked, and did a lot of drinking.

I would like to know why people have to make their enjoyment and fun someone else's problem. If people would take responsibility and practice the "do unto others" philosophy of life, then we wouldn't have to put up with the post-party evidence.

The students, especially, do not need to see that people come to the field to drink, smoke, party, and trash the grounds.

Obstacle

Avoiding the ugly sights of party leftovers.

Common Mistake

Allowing the students to see the post-party evidence. They don't need to see the carelessness and rudeness of others—especially when we try to tell them that people in sports should stay away from alcohol and drugs!

Solutions

- Check the grounds in the morning and clean up any mess that you don't want the students to be subjected to.
- If city league softball is played on the school field and this is a constant nuisance, call the parks and recreation department. Ask them to visit and enforce the no-alcohol, no-drugs rules.
- Call the police and ask if they would patrol at night.

Tips

- Use this as a teachable moment. Discuss the detrimental effects of using alcohol and drugs during sports and activities.

- Discuss how irritating it is to have people ruin your playing area. If you instill an attitude of respect for one's community, hopefully it will last throughout the students' lifetime and may rub off on the people around them.

Real-Life Story 📖

Corina jumped out of line, in a huff. She was mumbling and picking up cans from the field. The students' mouths dropped, and the teacher was bewildered. Corina said, "I told them before, not to dis our field. I can't believe they would do this. Wait till I see my uncle's softball team!" The other students picked up their chins and chipped in. Ah, good values at work.

IF IT HITS THE HIGHWAY, IT'S OUT

"OK, if the ball hits the curb, it's foul," states the leader of the group that is about to play kickball after school. "If it hits a tree, it's a double, but if it hits the highway, it's out and you're out." The new kid to the group asks, "Why is it out if it hits the highway? Shouldn't that be a home run?" The leader responds in an unfriendly tone: "No, dummy, if it hits the highway you can kiss the game and the ball away, because we can't cross the street, and the ball would get hit by the speeding cars."

If you're lucky, you'll have a large gym and an abundance of space in your fields for playing any activity. But for those physical education teachers without that luxury, we must modify and make do with what we've been given.

Your space might be limited, but don't let your mind be limited. Think of how you could modify each activity to fit your circumstances. Don't complain, but be thankful that you have something, however small it is.

Obstacle

Struggling with a small field space.

Common Mistakes

- Getting frustrated.
- Eliminating activities because of space restrictions.

Solutions

- Don't eliminate—modify.
- For a softball game, do the following:

    Shrink the base paths.

    Use a lighter ball (foam, rag, or Wiffle).

    Modify the boundaries.

    Turn the batter to a position in which he and the group would get the most out of the game (e.g., if you are facing houses, put the batter's back to the houses, so that a window doesn't get knocked out).

    Keep safety at the top of the lineup!

Tip

You can adjust any game in some manner to give the students at
least an introduction to the skills involved in the game.

Real-Life Story

A private Christian school was built on a two-lane, rarely traveled
road. The road became busier because the area around the school
grew. The school also grew and started to offer a physical education program. The only field space was in front of the school,
between it and the road. The school grew even more and started
a football team. One of the goal posts is 25 feet from the road. So
now, when a team has a field-goal kick, it needs a road-patrol
crossing guard to get the ball and to alert cars to flying footballs
that may hit their windows. The school kept growing despite the
obstacles.

"HAVE YOU BEEN ON VACATION?"

As you leisurely walk through school a fellow teacher stops you and asks, "Have you been on vacation?" You think, *When in the world could I have gone on vacation? I'm here every day teaching!* The teacher adds, "You look so tan!" You smile and say, "No, I haven't been on vacation, it's my job." She follows with, "What do you mean?" So you point outside to the clear, blue sky and say, "You know ... my job ... outside in the gorgeous sunshine every day." With confidence, you return to the gym, feeling healthy and alive.

Now you must wonder what they say about you when your hair has been battered about by the wind, your nose is running from the freezing temperatures, or you are sweaty and smelly from the heat.

Obstacle

None—you are one of the few lucky professionals who get the benefit of enjoying the sunshine and fresh air in the spring and summer!

Common Mistakes

- Not taking pleasure in the benefits of being the physical education teacher.
- Bragging during the nice-weather days. You know that if you boast now, you'd better not complain during the cold, wet, and freezing weather that you also will get (except for the lucky teachers who work with a year-round temperature between 60 and 90 degrees).
- Not wearing sunscreen.

Solution

Enjoy, enjoy, enjoy! Take this pleasure as your gift for doing a job that's very important in the lives of children.

Tips

- Remember above all that teaching, not tanning, is the physical education teacher's priority.

- Use sunblock or sunscreen and a hat to avoid overexposure to the sun.
- Always remember to keep the sun out of the students' eyes during a lesson.

Real-Life Story

A teacher was so engrossed in the physical fitness testing of her students that she didn't realize the burn that she had just received from the early March sun's rays. She was pink by noon. By 3:30 in the afternoon, she was a lobster! Once she realized that she was getting burned, it was difficult to avoid it. She had to face a certain way because of the testing situation and environment. She had not brought her sunscreen to school yet, and she had no hat. She had a date that night and could not hide her red nose and white eyes.

So be prepared and keep your lotion at school all year round. Having a hat handy at school is a great idea, too.

chapter

11

OFF THE FIELD: ISSUES AND OPPORTUNITIES

TIME-OUT

"Fun," "play," "sports," and "games" are all terms associated with physical education. That's one reason that some people think physical education is an easy subject to teach. They don't realize that you must maintain a good teaching atmosphere while working with students who are excited, running, playing, throwing, kicking, and striking objects in an environment filled with noise, smells, animals, bugs, and varying weather conditions. There are not four walls to confine a person, nor is there a chair to sit in a corner. So now try to conduct a good lesson while managing all the external, uncontrollable circumstances.

When a student is not on task, the physical education teacher must respond immediately and remedy the problem. "Time-out" is a good choice, if used properly.

Obstacle

Providing good classroom management with time-out.

Common Mistakes

- Putting a child in time-out and forgetting about her. This is an injustice. You want the student to get as much participation as possible!
- Using time-out too much.
- Allowing students to run amok, thus permitting an unsafe, uncontrollable environment.

Solutions

- Time-out is a winning solution because the students hate to be out, and they normally will do what they are supposed to do so they won't have to go into time-out.
- Let students know what behaviors will cause them to go into time-out.
- Let them know how to get out of time-out:

    They must understand what it was that put them in time-out.

    They should tell you what they did and how they will improve their behavior.

    They must agree not to do it again when they get out.

Tip

Keep your time-out student in clear view.

Real-Life Story

David knew immediately, when he was put in time-out, how to get released from it. He was very excitable and sometimes his inability to control his behavior would lead him to the time-out spot. David hated to lose a second of physical education, so he would regroup, explain to the teacher what he did wrong and how he would improve his behavior, get out as fast as he could, and stay out of time-out.

"NO BRAIN" ZONE

It's an unfair stereotype, but sometimes it is assumed that physical education teachers' intelligence is low. How low? Sometimes, the gauge might seem daunting to overcome.

Job	Intelligence zone level
Rocket Scientists	Out-of-this world smarts
Doctors	A healthy dose of smarts
Business professionals	Money = Smarts
Classroom teachers	Book smarts
Laborers	Street smarts
Physical education teachers	Sport smarts
No Brain Zone	Duh

Don't be offended. Different jobs come with different challenges, and some people are better suited to certain jobs. Ask a rocket scientist to handle 20 children on a rainy day with limited equipment, and she will likely pass that task right back to you. The physical education intelligence zone is farther removed from the "no brain" zone than some might think. Doing a good job is your chance to prove it.

Obstacle

Overcoming the physical education teachers' intelligence-zone stereotype.

Common Mistake

Letting the perceived physical education intelligence zone get to you.

Solutions

- Laugh—out loud! Don't let it get you down.
- Ignore the ignorance and get into the conversations at work that interest you. You soon will prove the people who believe the stereotypes wrong.
- Don't overdo it. If you try too hard to fit in, that will be detrimental for you. You'll set yourself off more. Just be yourself and don't try to force the others to change their minds about stereotypes; allow them to discover the truth for themselves.

Tip

For fun, surprise the critics in the lounge or a faculty meeting with your tactful display of knowledge about a subject that seems to have nothing to do with physical education. Watch the teachers' mouths drop.

Real-Life Story

For the first three months of school, the new physical education teacher, Ms. Lancaster, observed and took in all the newness of the school environment. She tried to be the best teacher that she could, while watching and learning from others. Then when she had gained confidence, she shocked the staff during a meeting as she gave them her intellectual input on how to improve math and language arts test scores. The things she said not only made sense but were great ideas! She jumped up at least three notches on the intellectual chart that day.

SUB IN HIGH HEELS

You've heard the sayings: "There's no substitute for a good teacher." "It's party time, we have a substitute today!" Or, "The class is crazy—they have a sub today."

It's hard enough to find a good substitute for a classroom teacher, but when a substitute is needed for a physical education teacher, it's even more challenging. When substitute teachers are called on the phone, most of them assume it is for a classroom. So when a substitute commits to a job, it doesn't always mean that she is ready for the position.

Some substitutes don't have the right clothes for physical education. Beware of the sub that you can hear coming down the hallway—because she has heels on, and she won't be ready to walk out onto the soft, dewy, wet fields. It also will be hard for her to demonstrate the "hike" with her dress on, how to field a ball, or many other skills involving movement.

Our dream is for the substitutes who bring their jogging outfit, whistle, sports bottle, sweatband, and stopwatch and are ready to go. But others are afraid to teach physical education. They will be faced with teaching a subject that they may not have any knowledge of. They will have weather issues as well as classroom management issues because the volume is louder and there are not four walls to contain the students. Most substitutes don't know how to teach physical education. However, subs are necessary and appreciated when the fit is a good one.

Obstacle

Surviving a substitute.

Common Mistakes

- Not informing the substitute about the position he is taking for the day. The physical education teacher may not do the recruiting but the administrator does, and hopefully she will tell the sub what he will be teaching.
- Not having good substitute plans.
- Not being organized.

Solutions

- Be organized—have a system. Have everything simply organized and laid out (schedule, seating arrangements, procedures).
- Create easy-to-understand lessons. Put everything in layperson, or "non-jock," terminology.
- Prepare students for a substitute teacher. Let them know at the beginning of the year your expectations and what they should expect with a sub. Review this with them when you have a scheduled absence.

Tips

Teach your students a game or fun activity that a substitute can do easily.

- Create a user-friendly "sub folder" before you begin the school year. In your sub folder, place your schedule, your roll sheets, your planned activities, some simple advice, your emergency information, a positive quote, and a thank-you note.
- Write your substitute a friendly, thankful letter and attach it to your sub folder.
- Ask a fellow teacher who knows your organization to check in with the sub in the morning.
- Leave candy!
- Be ready for the worst. Sometimes a physical education sub will only take the job as a last resort, and he'll hate every minute of it.
- Ask whoever's in charge of obtaining substitutes to tell the substitute the position that he'll be subbing for.
- Don't be disappointed. The sub is not you. She will not be able to ease through a lesson with 300 kids a day that she doesn't know.

Real-Life Story

The substitute comes down the hallway, clicking her heels, all dressed up and looking professional. When she realizes that the room number she is headed toward is the gym—"yikes!" She is about to cry, and then she has to laugh. She has made a commitment, and she is bound and determined to keep it. The sub takes each class outside, and she does the best that she can. By the end of the day, her heels are full of dried-up mud and her hose has grass stuck to them, but she has made it. The students aren't likely to forget it. They say that they treated her nicely because without her they wouldn't have had physical education that day.

NO TEACHER, NO SUB, NO CLASS

When you are absent from school, several things can happen. If your school values physical education and the teachers' schedule, it will get a substitute to replace you. If it gets a sub, the likelihood that she wants to teach physical education is slim: so your students end up not having a good class. If they get a substitute who thinks physical education is easy, then the students may take advantage of the sub and have an unsafe field day. If the school doesn't value physical education or has to pay for its own subs, physical education class might just be canceled altogether.

"Aw," sigh the students as they hear the bad news that physical education is canceled for the day. "Aw," sigh the classroom teachers as they hear the news that they will not be getting their 45-minute break today. "Aw," you sigh, because you feel sorry for the school, but you have to be out. This seems sad, but it really strengthens your position at the school. When you come back, everyone is elated because the students have their physical education time and trusted teacher back, the teachers get their break time back, and the nurse does not have to deal with so many injuries.

Obstacle

> When you have to be away from school, sometimes they will cancel your classes.

Common Mistake

> Worrying, instead of using it to your advantage.

Solutions

- If your administrator decides to cancel your classes, then you have no guilt or worry because it is not your doing. You must have days off for sickness and other things, but it's your principal or substitute finder's fault or concern for not securing a sub.

- Use this as a tool to show how important physical education is to the students, and you may get some extra support. Sometimes things will happen without anything being said.

- Definitely discuss the substitute issue with your principal.

Tips

- It could be that the principal doesn't trust a substitute to come into a high-risk subject and create chaos. So he chooses to cancel your classes instead.
- Whatever the reason, you've done your best to keep physical education going, so don't worry.
- Here's a chance for you to shine. Everyone misses you. This shows how important you are to the students and the flow of the schedule for the teachers.

Real-Life Story

A substitute had taken over for the sick physical education teacher one day. When the teacher got back to school, there was a long note on the desk. The frazzled replacement for the day had found out that the job of a physical education teacher shouldn't be taken for granted and that the students can misbehave and be unsafe. The physical education teacher smiled about the note and thought how tough it can be on a substitute and the students. Upon her return, she thoroughly enjoyed the hugs and "welcome backs" she warmly received for her one-day absence from the teachers, the principal, and, most of all, the students!

WHAT ARE SOLS?

SOLs: You have to teach them. You've heard about them. You've seen others worry about them. So what are they?

They are Standards of Learning—which each student in a certain grade level should be able to comprehend during the year. In other places, these may be referred to as Standards of Accreditation. In Virginia, where I teach, each teacher is accountable for teaching these standards. The teachers must teach the required Standards of Learning throughout the year. All of the standards for that level should be covered within the year. In some grades, the students are required to take SOL tests. The students and the schools are rated according to their scores on these tests.

These are a big deal! They also are very controversial. Some teachers feel as though they only can focus on SOLs, and it gets stressful. They think that the SOLs squash their creativity because they have to drill the students on them so much that they don't have time for anything else. Others view them as a guide to what they should be teaching.

Physical education teachers do have SOLs, or some standards that they must teach; however, the school system you are working in will decide whether you use them. If you don't have to use them, it is important to give support to the teachers who do. Physical education can assist in tackling the SOLs of other subjects as well the PE SOLs, by helping kids to understand and learn in a fun way.

Obstacle

Working with SOLs.

Common Mistakes

- Ignoring the SOLs.
- Thinking that they are not your problem.

Solutions

- Look at the SOLs as a framework to work within and go beyond. How much more can you successfully teach? Pack in the essentials plus extras for free. Make your lessons have a little bit more than what is called for by the SOLs. You may find that you can squeeze them in if you've planned them out already.

- Help the classroom teachers teach the SOLs by interlinking your lessons with a concept that an SOL is covering. Find out what the teachers are working on in class. Examples:

  If they are working on time, incorporate a math lesson into your physical education class as the students are performing races and reading a stopwatch. Running within a specified time, for the mile run or shuttle run on fitness tests, is a good method.

  If the students are studying Greece in social studies, do a unit on the Olympics and squeeze in information about Greek and Olympic history.

Tips

- Interlinking with the SOLs is fun for the students. It brings concepts to real life when they are done in physical education.
- If you knew how much your efforts help the students to "get" the concepts, you would link every lesson possible with an SOL.
- Don't forget, if you have SOLs—yours come first!
- Make sure when you are interlinking that you are making the link natural. A natural fit is what will make the lessons smooth.

Real-Life Story

Ms. Evans planned her physical education lessons carefully, to make each lesson as worthwhile as she could. She did a theme on the Olympics; this lasted for one month. She was able to include fitness concepts, throwing, catching, striking, kicking, tumbling, dancing, and dribbling skills in the unit. She also included geography by using the countries that would participate in the Olympics as teams. Student teams would get extra credit if they researched their country and shared it with the group. They used math with times, distances, adding, subtracting, measuring, and understanding when to use what concept. Vocabulary and foreign languages also were used. This was exciting not only for the students but for all the teachers involved. In the long run, the students had an appreciation for all the concepts and could apply them to the real world.

SCHEDULING NIGHTMARE

Here is Ms. Sanders's physical education schedule:

8:30–9:20 = eighth grade

9:20–10:10 = seventh grade

10:15–10:45 = kindergarten on Monday, Wednesday, and Friday

10:15–10:45 = preschool on Tuesday and Thursday

10:50–11:20 = second grade

11:25–11:55 = fifth grade

11:55–12:30 = lunch

12:30–1:00 = third grade

1:10–1:45 = fourth grade

1:55–2:25 = first grade

2:30–3:15 = sixth grade

3:15–3:30 = planning

If that isn't a chopped-up schedule, then what is? The seventh- and eighth-graders are back to back; then the teacher must quickly change gears and get into preschool/kindergarten mode. The whole schedule jumps up and down from grade to grade, without any changeover time. Can you find the planning time? Fifteen minutes uninterrupted and 10 minutes here and 5 minutes there make for useless time—and a situation in which you can't possibly plan.

Obstacle

Handling the nightmare schedule.

Common Mistake

Letting frustration get the best of the program.

Solutions

- Have a meeting about scheduling with your principal at the beginning of the school year and at the end. Discuss scheduling issues and requests.
- Always keep the meeting in a positive tone, even when speaking about the negative points.
- Explain the mental changeover needed to accommodate this schedule. Tell the principal that the changeover wouldn't be so bad once a day, but several times a day is draining.

- Explain the physical equipment changeover necessary for each grade.
- After putting up with this schedule for one year, proving that you can be open-minded and positive, politely request a change.

Tips

- If the schedule is overbearing and will not change after a year, and after a discussion with the principal, look for another school. There are many variations of physical education programs out there. Call around to other schools to find out more.
- Ask students to help you set up and break down for the next grade level.

Real-Life Story

Ms. Jackson worked hard with whatever came her way during her first year as a physical education teacher. She took whatever she got. At the end of the year she spoke about her requests for scheduling, and the principal was very receptive. Ms. Jackson designed her own schedule, and then the principal looked it over and approved it. Everything else was scheduled around physical education.

IT'S ONLY PHYSICAL EDUCATION

"Bradley?" calls out the physical education teacher as she takes roll. She hears no answer.

"Bradley?" she calls out again the next time she has Bradley's class. Again there is no answer.

"Bradley?" she calls the next time, as she looks around to see if he is there. "What is going on with Bradley?"

It's been a month and she hasn't seen that great little student in class. When physical education class only meets once a week, this is detrimental to the absent student and to the teacher's record keeping and unit planning.

Why did Bradley miss so much? Well, he was sick one day, another day he went to strings class, another day his classroom teacher needed some students to help her with a project, and one day was a holiday. So Bradley missed the throwing introduction lesson, the revisiting lesson, and the game lesson. The problem isn't Bradley—he loves physical education. The problem is the perception of physical education. People think that physical education is a fun, nonserious subject, that it doesn't teach anything, and that it can be missed by students. Physical education is used by many teachers as a reward to get students to behave well. They tell students that if they misbehave they will be unable to go to PE. Many administrators, teachers, and parents will not see physical education as an important subject. To them, "it's only PE."

Obstacle

Overcoming the attitude that physical education doesn't matter

Common Mistakes

- Buying into that same way of thinking
- Taking it easy, and just rolling out the ball because you're tired of trying
- Causing people to think this way because of the way your program is designed

Solutions

Always remember the following:

Your program matters!

Your program has substance!

Your program makes a difference!

Your program teaches skills, concepts, vocabulary, math, social studies, psychology, sociology, health, and science—all wrapped into a fun little package called physical education. Know this, teach this, push this!

Only you can convince others how important your subject is to students.

Strive for equality. People should do unto physical education as they would do unto their own area of specialty.

Let the faculty and families of your school know how important physical education is, not just by telling them but by proving it through your actions.

Bring concerns up at faculty meetings. Be ready to hear the negative and the positive.

The biggest advocate for your program is your student body. If the students think PE is worthwhile, then that is what matters. They will spread the word.

Tips

- If you make missing physical education not a big deal, then everyone else will, too.
- Use assessment to show the need to have students in class when scheduled.

Real-Life Story

Each time Ms. Whitmore's class would come to physical education there would be about 10 students. That would mean that only 10 people would get the warm-up and introduction. Then a student would wander outside to class and come up to the physical education teacher and ask what she should do. Another student would come speeding out of the gym doors, raring to go, and ask the teacher what to do. The students would trickle outside bit by bit, until a total of 25 students would finally all be accounted for in class. What did their classroom teacher think? The fact is, Ms. Whitmore didn't think at all about so many students missing an important lesson. Nor did she think about how the physical education teacher felt having to explain the lesson over and over again.

The physical education teacher figured out this trend and discussed the concern firmly, yet positively, with Ms. Whitmore. Ms. Whitmore had never considered physical education to be important until someone confronted her and explained the issues to her. Her students now show up on time, and all together, ready to learn something every day.

COMMUNICATION

When you have your program designed for the year, do you just sit back in your office and let the year take off? Sure, you've planned, and gotten your lessons ready, and you're going to have a great time when the students come to class.

Being a quality physical education teacher will take more than just teaching a good lesson for 45 minutes. It's going to take communication. Communication with kids, parents, fellow teachers, principals, supervisors, communities, and the public is essential for a truly good, "quality" physical education program.

If you don't communicate, your program will die. Communication will help make your program thrive. Thrive? Die? Which will you choose?

Obstacle

Making sure your program is thriving through communication.

Common Mistakes

- Living in your own little physical education world, only worried about yourself.
- Thinking that you don't need to communicate. If you don't communicate, how will people know how important physical education is in school? They may think it is a waste of time, and they may try to delete it.

Solutions

- Be positive in every aspect of communicating—even if what you are communicating is negative or not such great news.
- Communicate at the beginning of the year by discussing your yearly plans with the principal and other teachers.
- Ask how you can incorporate other subjects within your physical education units.
- At the beginning of the year, send a letter to the parents describing your program and follow it up with a physical education newsletter (see sample newsletter on next page).
- Send out colorful, clear flyers to promote any program.
- Talk to the students about the exciting things you are doing in PE.
- Call your local newspaper and list any noteworthy events and happenings in physical education.

HOLLAND ELEMENTARY SCHOOL PHYSICAL EDUCATION NEWSLETTER

March–April edition

INTERLINKING TO THE CORE!

The Holland PE program desires to help each student with skill and physical development, as well as linking the core subjects to physical education. Check out the math in March Madness and social studies in the Olympics in early April. We would love to link into what you are covering your class. Just pass the word and we'll work it in.

RECESS

If you are frustrated over students whining about the disappearance of playground equipment, don't lose hope. There is equipment on the way for each grade level. If you need something in the meantime, see Ms. Sutherland in advance to check out PE equipment.

MARCH MADNESS

Our students love to participate in basketball-type activities. In celebration of the NCAA basketball tournament, we are going to create a math skills tournament at Holland. We will be graphing, estimating, predicting, and using many math skills while following the tournament. Mr. McIntyre will provide the daily rundown of happenings to the students.

We will provide you with information to get involved.

THANK YOU! Thanks for all the support you provide for the PE program.

*—Ms. Sutherland
and the PE Crew*

- List happenings in physical education in your faculty report letters.
- When a student is doing poorly, communicate by using these methods:

   Send a note home, starting with a positive note first.

   Call home to keep an open line of communication.

   Ask for conferences, and invite the principal and other teachers.

- Document your communications with others.
- Keep an open mind.
- Keep up with current physical education innovations, trends, and changes.

Tips

- Keep physical education positive.
- Promote physical education every chance you get.

Real-Life Story

Every few years physical education seems to come up for a review in the education department. If physical education isn't considered worthwhile or important, then it makes the "chopping block" list. Then a whole bunch of physical education advocates have to rally together to keep the program going. Don't let it get to that point! Don't leave any doubt in people's minds that physical education is important. If you constantly communicate this, then there will not be a crisis every few years.

THE FACULTY MEETING

Although you don't sit in a classroom all day long, safely behind a desk, inside the comfort of four walls, you are part of the school faculty. You may be unlike the classroom teachers, or you just happen to teach a subject that is very different from most of the teachers in your school. You may even think you have very little in common with this group, but you are a part of the team and have more in common than you realize. Regardless of your perspective on where you fit in, you do fit in here. You are the physical education teacher. As a part of the faculty, you will need to attend faculty and staff meetings.

Obstacle

Sitting through a boring faculty meeting that has little or nothing to do with your subject.

Common Mistakes

- Not attending the meeting.
- Napping at the meeting.

Solution

Go, without a second thought, to every single meeting!

Tips

- Reasons why you should never miss a faculty meeting:

  The meeting you miss will be the one in which they nominate you for cafeteria/lunch duty because you are "good with loud noises."

  Your faculty and staff may decide to use the gym for strings, band classes, and storage because most of the time you are outside for physical education class anyway. Since you don't attend the meeting, someone may speak for you and say he's sure you wouldn't mind.

It will be totally your fault if you miss a deadline or an opportunity.

Food might be served.

- Reasons why you always want to attend:

This is your chance to talk up and sell your program. Get the whole school involved in physical education. This keeps you and the faculty and staff in touch with each other. This also will make you look good in front of your principal!

Look at each meeting as if you are playing a game. You are part of the defensive team. You are there to defend your goal (your physical education goals). If you're not there, covering, you know someone will attack.

You want to be part of the team, and lead by example. The team plays better if all the key players show up.

Real-Life Story

Mrs. Colter had a doctor's appointment on the day of the faculty meeting. She intentionally scheduled the appointment at this time to avoid the dull, drawn-out meeting. The meetings were such a waste of her time, she thought, and they almost always had nothing to do with her program. She skipped the meeting and created a story to tell her principal to cover the fact that she intentionally made the appointment to conflict with the meeting.

When Mrs. Colter arrived at school the next day, she went to check in and when she looked in her mailbox, she discovered a copy of the schedule for the upcoming school year. She had been given first grade first thing in the morning at 8:00, followed by a three-minute break and then fifth grade. Fifth grade was followed by four classes in a row with three minutes in between. Lunch didn't come until 1:00 for 30 minutes. Fourth grade came next, followed by a 10-minute planning period, and the day ended with the weary kindergartners for 30 minutes.

Mrs. Colter's new schedule had no solid setup or changeover time for the different grade levels. The planning was so chopped up that it was hard to figure out the 45 minutes a day that she was given to plan. She also had to watch how much water she drank because those three precious moments between classes would be soaked up by the picking up and dropping off of students. Mrs. Colter complained about the teachers who took advantage of her absence in making the schedule. The bottom line was that she hadn't been at the meeting, and she was told that it was the only way they could possibly work everyone into the schedule.

You better believe that Mrs. Colter did not miss another faculty meeting!

"IT'S MY WAY OR A LAWSUIT"

Sadly, we live in a litigious world. We unfortunately are living in a world where we are not immune to the word "sue." What a shame that we can't do some of the really fun things anymore because people are afraid of being sued. No more trampolines, no more gymnastics in some schools, no hockey sticks, no diving, no diving boards, no slides ... and so on. It's not worth the risk!

That's why some people have jobs called "risk management." What they do for their companies is they make sure that the company is not in danger of being sued, they check out claims, and they prevent risks from becoming potential money losses.

Guess where the most liability exists within a school? In physical education class. Throwing objects, objects flying through the air, striking objects, tagging and touching others, wide-open spaces—these all are potential hazards. It takes a good physical education teacher to minimize the risks and create a solid and safe program.

So you have a principal or superintendent who is petrified of physical education's potential for risk and injury. He has told you what you can and cannot do, and the list of "cannots" is double that of the "cans." When you question the man in charge, he says, "It's either my way, or a lawsuit." Your questioning must stop there! Now prove your safety record and prove that physical education is worthwhile and not just a risk.

Obstacle

> Working with a skeptical administrator/principal concerned with your program's safety.

Common Mistakes

- Ignoring the warnings and limitations from the people in charge of making decisions.
- Making foolish, risky decisions to please yourself.

Solutions

- Prove yourself.
- Prove your judgment.
- Prove your teaching and planning ability.
- Document, document, document. It can't be emphasized enough. Whatever happens, write it down, and date it, with witnesses.

- Create plans using skills and methods appropriate for the grade level and experience level of the students you are working with.
- Write clear, complete lesson plans, with the appropriate information listed (see lesson plan):

    List the skill you will be covering (e.g., throwing).

    List the focus—what part of the skill, when you break it down, will you zero in upon (e.g., overhand throw to target)?

    List a cue—how can you make the action of the skill simple to perform and the use easy to remember, with catchy terms or phrases (e.g., "hand by the ear," "listen to the ball")?

    List what grades the lesson addresses.

    List interlinks—what other subject areas will combine with this lesson (e.g., running the mile involves math/time)?

    List the necessary equipment and how many of each you will need.

    List the objective—what is it that you want to accomplish in this lesson?

    List the warm-up—what quick stretch or activity will you have the students do to get ready for the lesson?

    Describe the introduction—how you entice the students to want to participate in the activity. Create an inviting statement or question to lead into your activity.

    Describe the activity—how the area will be set up, how far apart one thing will be from another, any safety precautions for setup, how the students will be positioned, the name of the activity, how the students accomplish the objective, what you would like the students to do, and how they play.

    Explain your assessment—how you will measure what the students have learned (e.g., teacher observation, peer assessment, participation).

    Explain your closure—how you bring the lesson to a close, stating the objective, asking the students what they learned, and telling them what to expect next class.

    Make your evaluation—notes for yourself, about how the lesson went, where you left off, or ideas to change.

Table 11.1 **Physical Education Lesson Plan**

Skill: _____

Focus/cue: _____

Teacher: _____

Grades: _____

Interlink: _____

Area: _____

Equipment: _____

Objective: _____

Period breakdown

1. Warm-up (7 minutes) _____

2. Introduction (1 minute) _____

3. Activity (30 minutes) _____

4. Safety precautions _____

5. Assessment
   • Teacher observation _____
   • Self-assessment _____
   • Participation _____

6. Conclusion (1 minute) _____

7. Evaluation _____

- Communicate with your supervisors. Ask for chances to prove yourself.
- Join a physical education organization and keep up with current safety issues, changes and innovations. Here are a few suggestions:

    The American Alliance for Health, Physical Education, Recreation and Dance (AAHPERD)

    The state AHPERD chapter (e.g., in Virginia, it's VAHPERD)

    The National Alliance of Youth Sports

    The National Association for Sport and Physical Education (NASPE)

    The American Alliance for Active Lifestyles and Fitness

    Sportsmedia Mailing List

- Make sure you are acting as a reasonably prudent and fair physical education teacher.

Tip

If your child were attending your school, would you be comfortable and secure with the teacher doing the activities in the manner that you are doing them? If so, then you are probably doing everything reasonably and safely! Just remember to continue to self-evaluate and stay on top of safety issues.

Real-Life Story

Mr. Saddle, the physical education teacher, did not comply with the standards that his supervisor set up for his program, and year after year he did his own thing. One year a student got severely hurt during an activity that was forbidden by the supervisor. When the school was sued, the principal and supervisor did not stand behind

Mr. Saddle, because he was at fault for not following procedure. The school system had to pay out a lot of money, because Mr. Saddle did not have enough money for a lawsuit. He was fired from his job. Everyone in the school system loses in this type of incident. Don't let it happen to you.

c h a p t e r

12

BECOMING
A BETTER
TEACHER

DON'T TURN YOUR BACK

The very moment you turn your back, a student may attempt to do something unacceptable just because he thinks he can get away with it. You remember what it was like when you had an ineffective teacher: your class was more out of control, and you didn't have the environment needed to learn at your optimum level.

I love to watch teachers who lead their line and keep their back to the class, as they walk ahead of the students who are jumping, hitting, and running around playing tag. They are so oblivious to what's going on that they are actually inviting poor behavior from their students. Then they turn around in a huff and yell at their class for its actions.

A few simple classroom management techniques and strategies should always be taken into consideration when teaching.

Obstacle

Preventing potential behavior problems.

Common Mistakes

- Not preventing but reacting.
- Providing an environment that allows students to misbehave.

Solutions

Put the following strategies into practice:

- Keep your back to the wall: keep your eyes on all the children so that no student is behind your back. Once a child thinks you can't see her, it's "party time!"
- Don't turn your back: while walking a line of students somewhere, always walk in the back, making sure that all students know that you're there and you're watching them.
- Be on the ball: know what's going on in class by scanning, looking, and listening. Stay with it.
- Create the "desire to please": if the students know they can please you, and that you will reward them with your praise, then they will behave in order to get that praise.

Tip

If you set the tone to do what's right and to provide everyone with a great time, and you combine that with the techniques mentioned, then you almost always will have success.

Real-Life Story

Ms. Runner was not the mothering type of teacher, nor the easy teacher, nor even the funniest teacher, but everyone wanted to be in her class for physical education. Why? Because she set a positive tone in which everyone wanted to do what was right in order to please her, and in return, the students would get to do more activities and receive positive feedback. Ms. Runner was fair, she talked with enthusiasm, she got to the point, and she established a positive classroom environment. She told her students what she expected, and then she made the expectations reachable and desirable. The students were aware of procedures, rules, consequences, and opportunities. She would review these often. So the students enjoyed her class, and so did Ms. Runner.

"HEY, CAN YOU HEAR ME?"

"Ms. Stevens. Hey, Ms. Stevens. Hey, Ms. Stevens. Ms. Stevens! Hey, Ms. Stevens!" calls a nagging student who wants attention. She purposely ignores him and carries on with her demonstration of catching with a lacrosse stick, so that the student does not interrupt the flow of her class.

"Can I come back? I'll be good. Please, Ms. Stevens. Can you hear me?" cries out the student who really wants her to pay him some attention, because he is dying to grab that lacrosse stick and catch that ball. Some students will nag and nag until you respond to them. Other students will just cry. Some students will throw a fit to try and force you to pay attention to them. Then there are others who will sit nicely and do their time until you are ready to respond to them.

Obstacle

Handling the nagging students who want your attention but don't know how to get it properly.

Common Mistakes

- Allowing their annoyance to interrupt your lesson.
- Pacifying them, by stopping your lesson to respond to another interruption from the student.

Solutions

- Use the "selective ignoring" technique. Obviously, the student already has misbehaved somehow, so if you give in to him this time, you will be allowing him to interrupt your instruction again. Unless the students are injured, they will be fine sitting there until you are ready to respond.
- Use nonverbal communication to signal to the student to be quiet, and wait for a moment.
- Always keep one eye on the students who are sitting out.
- Let all students, including the person sitting out, hear you say, "Anytime a student is interrupting a teacher while instructing, they are being disrespectful and will not get the attention any faster than the respectful person who is being patient and good. The respectful person will get the kind of attention you want. No one wants negative attention." Then carry on with your instruction.

Tip

Do not let the student see you getting aggravated. He will think he is manipulating you and he knows he still is getting your attention. He will enjoy the attention that the class is giving him, too.

Real-Life Story

While Joshua was sitting in time-out for misbehaving, he just about drove himself crazy. He knew what he had done wrong and wanted to tell the teacher so that he could do the right thing and participate. Unfortunately, he yelled for attention, and then he started jumping, and when that didn't work, he started to do cartwheels. He knew that he would get attention, and he was hoping to then get back in the activity. What Joshua wasn't counting on was the extra discipline for disrespect and dangerous behavior. As soon as the lacrosse catching technique was finished, and the other students had begun catching, the teacher visited Josh. She increased his time-out sentence and he had to discuss his dangerous behavior with his teacher. Once Joshua realized that his teacher only responded positively to positive behavior, he did just fine.

"HOORAY, WE'RE RUNNING""OH, NO, WE'RE RUNNING"

"Hooray, we're running!" David exclaims, pumping his fist and arm as he enters the gym. "Oh, no, we're running," Brittany sighs, as she drops her shoulders and enters the gym.

Some people will enjoy running and some people won't. As an athlete, you probably can't escape running. We've all had coaches or physical education teachers who have used running as a punishment. No doubt, running can make you feel pain. A lot of pain! So for those people who don't enjoy it, and don't have mental toughness, running is a dreaded chore.

To the others, running is freedom and release—it's stress relieving, addicting, and exciting. These students love to run as much as they can. They know the reward you get from the second wind and the way your body feels after finishing a good run!

Watch out, because when these kids are running that's all they are thinking about. If they are running in a lesson, you might as well have up a "beware, kids running" sign. Running can be so fun if it's designed to be fun.

Obstacle

Overcoming the dread of running, and making it the pleasure of running.

Common Mistakes

- Using running as a punishment.
- Not making running fun.
- Being repetitive.
- Taking the easy way out: "OK, kids, run a lap" is the easiest, and laziest, way to get kids to warm up and do a cardiovascular workout.

Solutions

- Be creative.
- Design warm-ups that include running and are fun.
- Organize tag games, silly races, or running while performing a skill (e.g., dribbling a soccer ball or basketball, or balancing a ball on a paddle, or tossing a ball to a partner or to oneself).
- Have students do instant activities that combine running and skills.

- Have a sign at the front of the gym instructing students what to do:

    "Run around and 'high-five' as many people as you can."

    "Run backward around the basketball court."

    "Follow the leader to the backstop and back."

    "Run around the bases, and see how many runs you can score before the time is up."

- Have students run with a purpose:

    To beat a certain time.

    To see how much distance they can cover in a certain amount of time.

    To beat a teacher's time in a fun run—in which the teacher runs and the students attempt to beat her (these are really exciting; sometimes you even can have the principal or another adult there to encourage the students to run faster).

- Organize scavenger hunts. Have the students run with a group or partner to reach a given goal by finding certain items.

- Whatever you do, keep it exciting.

Tip

You know how you get about the "same old, same old." The kids are the same. So give running a little spice.

Real-Life Story

The students at Century Elementary didn't like physical education much. There were more sick notes from children at that school than at any other school. No one from the outside could figure out why a child wouldn't love physical education. After the program was investigated, it was found that every single day the students did 10 minutes worth of stretching and calisthenics and then did a run. The run was a quarter-mile: some kids finished in two minutes, while others took six. Then the students would only have 10 minutes to learn a skill and perform the activity. This structured program never changed. The lack of variety, the monotony, turned off students. They would rather be creative in their imagination, sitting on the sidelines, than to do the same boring thing over and over again.

"WATCH ME, LOOK AT ME"

"Hey, Ms. Aris, watch me. Hey, Ms. Aris, watch me, Ms. Aris. Ms. Aris, look, look, watch this!" "Ms. Aris, would you please come watch me throw this ball?" "Look, come see me—look, Ms. Aris."

These are not exaggerations. They are genuine comments that physical education teachers hear over and over. Of course, as soon as you see the child perform after she's been chanting to you for five minutes, her throw doesn't hit the target but instead nearly hits the student beside her. Now, the student has to wait for you to go around the class again before she can try to impress you once more.

Some people might really tire of this if they were to hear it six hours a day. It's like, "Mom, Mom, Mom, watch me, Mom—Mom!" or, "Dad, hey Dad, look, Dad—Dad!" at home. Some teachers may say to the persistent student, "Do not call for me any more! You're driving me crazy!"

But not a quality physical education teacher. Quality PE teachers would realize how excited these students are about what you've asked them to do. They are performing for you—just for you. Wow, that's invigorating! What an honor to have someone want to do something just for you. This is one of the reasons we're teaching physical education. What we quality PE teachers ultimately strive for is that these students learn physical skills and get excited about what we're teaching them.

Obstacle

Handling all those requests for your attention.

Common Mistake

Thinking that the students are really bothering you, and allowing this to annoy you.

Solutions

- Strive for this sort of eager behavior from your students. This is what you want from them—that they show you how proud they are that they can perform a skill well and that you've taught them. How gratifying!

- Have a positive word for every student who calls for you:

    "Good job!"

    "Nice try."

"Way to go!"

"You are improving. I like your enthusiasm."

Tip

Strive to get to this point. If you can get the students that motivated, you can teach them anything.

Real-Life Story

Mrs. Moore heard the students calling for her and she couldn't stand the nagging calls for her attention. She looked at it in a negative way instead of positive. She snapped at the students, "For God's sake, stop calling my name! I'll look at you when I am ready. Just do what you are told and don't bother me." Now when the students are excited, they certainly don't let her know, and all the enthusiasm is gone. Now the students don't perform for Mrs. Moore because they don't think she really wants to see them try or improve. When Mrs. Moore lost the students' enthusiasm, she also lost a lot more: the students' desire to do well for the teacher. This makes her job 10 times more difficult because they are not as interested or motivated to please.

"WHERE'S YOUR WHISTLE?"

"Tweeeet." "Get your butt moving—I don't want to hear any excuses." "Tweeeeeeeeeeet." "Run; don't walk like a sissy. Run, boy!"

Can you picture this guy? A big man with a scowl on his face, as he blows his whistle to get attention from the students in his class. Then he belts out mean and rude comments. Is this a quality physical education teacher? No, this is a stereotype of what a physical education teacher is. Hopefully, this is not you.

Many people think that physical education teachers must always carry a whistle. Why do you use a whistle? Mainly it's to make a loud enough noise that everyone can hear, because your voice isn't loud enough. In competitive games such as volleyball, basketball, and football, it stops the action momentarily. There are times for a physical education teacher to use a whistle, but in most cases the teacher should be using his voice.

If students respond to your voice, you won't have a need for the whistle. If you blow the whistle to make the students stop, listen, change directions, or line up, then they won't listen to your voice. Your class, because of its nature, will be loud, but don't rely on the whistle—it will take away from your effectiveness to communicate.

Obstacle

Communicating without relying on a whistle.

Common Mistake

Counting too much on the whistle to start, stop, and command attention.

Solutions

- Use your voice to communicate. That's what you want the students to focus on anyway.
- You are much more effective with the response to your voice than to a whistle. The students will start to tune out your voice and only respond to a loud whistle. If you lose that response, then you'll lose the effectiveness to have students tuned into your voice to direct them.
- If you are used to a whistle, try weaning yourself off it, a little bit at a time.

- All physical education teachers should have possession of a whistle for games and very large events. Sometimes, using a whistle, drum, musical instrument, megaphone, or music is fun for the students.

Tip

Keep a whistle in your desk drawer. The people who stereotype will always expect a physical education teacher to have a whistle. So, be prepared for any requests that might come your way for a whistle.

Real-Life Story

Mr. Atkins constantly blew his whistle every day. He used it for starting, stopping, listening, getting students to look at him, quieting the class, and everything else. One day Mr. Atkins got up late and rushed to school and forgot his whistle. It was chaos during class. The students didn't listen to him yelling, because they just weren't used to focusing on his voice. He shouted and hollered all day. He went home an absolute wreck! Mr. Atkins realized, then, not only how much he relied on his whistle, but also how much the students didn't listen to him and only listened to the whistle.

ADAPT AND ADJUST

Puddles, lawn-mower men, and special events may make you change your plans for a lesson, but sometimes you'll have to adapt and adjust to situations on a daily basis.

You might have a student or a whole class that has a disability. The disability will prevent some students from performing an activity the way an average person would. Do you just ignore these students and have them sit and watch?

What if the student has a leg brace but can still run? What if the student has a temporary cast or bandage? What if the student is in a wheelchair and functions on a one-year-old level? You need to think about what you would do in these situations.

Obstacle

> Adapting to disabilities and concerns that will require adjusting your lessons.

Common Mistakes

- Excluding students from the lesson.
- Ignoring students who can't perform activities.
- Not researching the concerns.
- Not counting your blessings.

Solutions

- Provide the least restrictive environment (LRE) possible for such students. In physical education, the LRE means that the student is placed where his disability does not prevent him from receiving quality instruction. If John was in a special education class because he had Down's syndrome, the school would place him into your regular physical education class to allow him to participate along with the other students.
- The appropriate measures should be followed with any student you must adapt to:

  > Does the student have an Individualized Education Plan (IEP)? By law, the IEP must include physical education. The IEP will state whether the student shall receive special services or special provisions for participating in class. Read the IEP.

  > Talk to the classroom teacher, parent, nurse, and principal about the student's limitations and abilities.

Figure out if the student is safe performing the activity.

Do you have an adapted physical education specialist in your school system? If so, contact that person with all concerns about disabilities and limitations of students.

Evaluate whether you are teaching so that each student can learn.

Talk to the student in question, and find out from her own mouth how she feels about physical education and what her limitations are.

- Read up on the laws:

Good information can be found in *Adapted Physical Activity, Recreation and Sport*, by Claudine Sherrill, Brown & Benchmark Publishers.

PL 94-142: The Education for All Handicapped Children Act. This ensures a right to a free education, a right to an appropriate education, a right to due process of the law, a right to nondiscrimination, and a right to be educated in the least restrictive environment.

PL 101-336: Americans With Disabilities Act (ADA). This law states that people with disabilities should have equal access and equal service as others. This would mean that for physical education teachers, our gyms and playgrounds and fields should provide equal access for those with disabilities. Most of the time, this obstacle can be overcome by a little extra attention and effort being placed in helping all students, not just the average ones.

Tips

- Do your homework.
- Make students feel good about themselves in physical education class, whether they are the star athlete or have a disability.
- Include students whenever possible.
- Never exclude.

Real-Life Story

Are you familiar with the title character from the movie *Forrest Gump*? Now, Forrest isn't a "real-life" story, but the intent of the filmmakers was to give us a protagonist from whom we could gain a lot of inspiration.

chapter

13

SPECIAL DAY
CHALLENGES

FIRE DRILL

The physical education teacher was demonstrating to her students as she explained, "Throw the ball to your partner and then. ..." A loud buzzing sound interrupted her, and the startled students began exclaiming, "Whoa! What do we do?" The fire-drill buzzer continued to emit the loud noise into the air, making the kids jump, shake, and scream.

Once the students had settled down, they began to quietly focus on their teacher and put down their equipment; they exited through the designated door and moved away from the building. This would not have been so smooth if they had not practiced and known what to do.

Sure, it's a little disruption in your day, but it's a necessary one.

Obstacle

Changes in plans due to necessary drills.

Common Mistakes

- Letting your students get out of control.
- Looking at the drill as a burden.
- Not taking the drill seriously.

Solutions

- Practice before you have your first drill. Discuss the importance of having a plan and executing it properly. There is more than one type of drill—there's the fire, the tornado, and the bomb drill. Your school may have even more. Treat these very seriously!
- Do not allow anyone to talk, goof off, or distract others.
- Make the most out of the drill. Make it into an action activity. Once the students hear the buzzer, they:

  jump once;

  look around from right to left, then focus on the teacher;

  pretend they are in a movie or television show and quickly tiptoe without saying a word; and

  stay one behind the other, with equal space between each other.

- Treat the drill seriously, yet make it exciting and important at the same time. If your students can't handle the excitement, do not play the movie or TV action activity.

- If you are outdoors, do the drills the same, but have the students hurry to the teacher from wherever they are on the field.

Tip

You could always do a fun activity relating to fire, firefighters, tornadoes, and weather-related emergencies. It is great when you can coordinate your activities with the months that recognize events. Many school calendars list the unique events. A few examples are Bus Safety Week, Fire Safety Week, and Safe Schools Week.

Real-Life Story

The warm-ups for the week at Dutch Elementary School were all related to drills that are held throughout the year. Some of the warm-ups involved tagging, dodging, chasing, freezing, and listening and responding to signals that the students needed to know about. This was a fun way to address the subject as a lead-in to a serious matter. It also prepared the students to be ready to respond to the actual drill when it occurred.

"WE'RE DOING WHAT FOR PE?"

"Only 10 more minutes till PE!" says Tim, smiling, as he looks at the clock and passes the information along to a classmate. "Yeah, I can't wait to see what we are going to do today. I hope we get to throw the footballs!" the other classmate replies excitedly. The teacher finally finishes talking and then says, "Let's line up for PE, class."

Once the students are in the gym, they huddle around Mr. McDonald and wait for the exciting news about the activity they'll be doing today. Anxiously awaiting the announcement, the students start to imagine the fun activities possible. Then Mr. McDonald begins to speak and all eyes are fixed on his face with great anticipation. "Today," he says, "we were going to enjoy quarterback completion, which is a cool throwing and catching game—like the NFL, but without tackling. Unfortunately, we have an interruption in our schedule."

The students hear the "cool" event planned and can't wait to grab a football and start. They hear the good news, and they only focus on that. The students listen restlessly to Mr. McDonald as he says, "Yes, I'm afraid we will have to postpone quarterback completion until next time because we have to go to an assembly at this time."

Smiles fall, heads drop, and disappointed sighs spread throughout the class. "We're doing what for PE?" says Tim. Students are grumbling: "I hate when this happens—why do we have to go to this stupid assembly, anyway?" "How come they always do them at PE time? I hate missing PE!"

Obstacle

Dealing with interruptions to the physical education schedule.

Common Mistakes

- Getting angry.
- Not accounting for this in the yearly plan.
- Not communicating with the people who schedule assemblies.

Solutions

- Accept the fact that interruptions will happen. They will happen more in your class because your subject, physical education, is not considered a core subject like math, English, science, or social studies.

- Account for interruptions. Make a schedule, but plan for interruptions at least monthly. If you plan a "fun day," and you lose physical education one day, slip it into the "fun day" slot.
- Ask the principal and the coordinator of the special events if they could rotate times and dates so that the same class doesn't always miss out on physical education. Otherwise, that group of students would be out of whack with the other classes.
- Be flexible. If you're not, you shouldn't be a physical education teacher. You only will get angry and burned out, and the students will be miserable, too.
- Use this as an assessment tool to see whether the students are enjoying your class.

Tips

- Make the most of what you've been given. If the students have to miss physical education for an assembly, in their next class tie in the physical education lesson with the assembly. Talk about how physical education interlinks with everything.
- Having an assembly is a good way for the students to realize how much they love physical education.
- Try not to mention what the students are missing in physical education class while attending the assembly. They may get angry and tune out an important message or presentation.

Real-Life Story

On several occasions the third-graders lost physical education class because of an assembly. The following year, when those students were in the fourth grade, the time frame for physical education was entirely the opposite of the previous year. One fourth-grader remarked to the physical education teacher, "I sure am glad we have PE first thing in the morning because that 1:00 spot always blocked us from getting our PE when there was an assembly."

FIELD DAYS

Laughing, playing, running, and competing are the signs of Field Day. Field Day is the most fun day of the year!

Obstacle

Having the best Field Day ever.

Common Mistake

Stressing out. Don't do it—just have fun!

Solutions

- Enjoy creating a fun day of fitness and physical skill.
- You could have a simple, fun day of play; you could put a lot of competition in your day; or you could have a theme. (Check "Field Day Ideas" for suggestions, pages 221-224.)
- Plan way ahead! This will reduce stress. Here are some things to think about:

  Costs

  Awards

  How many hours

  Snacks

  T-shirts

  Equipment

  Volunteers

  Theme

  Heat

  Water

- Prepare your students for what to expect.
- Prepare and motivate teachers and staff for this "awesome" day.
- Make sure you include the following people in your planning:

  Nurse—you could even bring the nurse to the field with you.

  Cafeteria workers—they could prepare bag lunches that the students eat outside like a picnic.

  Custodian—get extra trash cans and his cooperation.

  Faculty and staff—those without a homeroom class can help with the day's events.

Parents—let them know what is going on; they will be excited for their children and may wish to join them for the day.

PTA—this group may want to donate time or money.

Community—the military often wants to help out, and the people in the community may want to get involved with their local school.

Tips

- Keep the fun tradition going with changing themes (see "Field Day Ideas" section on "Field Day Themes," pages 222-224).
- Take slides of the fun events and create a slide show.
- Use a camcorder to make video tapes of the events.
- Sell inexpensive (e.g., $5) T-shirts to raise money for Field Day and other physical education expenses.

Real-Life Story

In all of the Field Days I have organized, I have yet to meet a student who does not like Field Day. This event is a break from the usual day, and the kids get to move around for a long time instead of sitting at their desks.

FIELD DAY IDEAS

Option 1: Fun for All

Everyone will enjoy this day together as a class. Each class will rotate from one event to another on a timed signal. This is good for team building and keeps the students together and controlled, and it keeps the teachers in proximity to the students and gets them involved.

Here is an example:

Teacher	8:30	8:45	9:00	9:15	9:30	9:45	10:00	10:15	10:30	10:45	11:00
Smith	A	B	C	D	E	F	G	H	I	J	K
Brown	B	C	D	E	F	G	H	I	J	K	A
Cooper	C	D	E	F	G	H	I	J	K	A	B
Jones	D	E	F	G	H	I	J	K	A	B	C
Little	E	F	G	H	I	J	K	A	B	C	D
Johnson	F	G	H	I	J	K	A	B	C	D	E
Wright	G	H	I	J	K	A	B	C	D	E	F
Williams	H	I	J	K	A	B	C	D	E	F	G
Blair	I	J	K	A	B	C	D	E	F	G	H
Clark	J	K	A	B	C	D	E	F	G	H	I
Rogers	K	A	B	C	D	E	F	G	H	I	J

Notes: Letters signify the different events. Students should rotate on the PE teacher's signal.

Option 2: Competitive Fun

This Field Day allows the students to work at their own pace while having a common goal in mind for the team or class. The students attempt to complete every single event in a given amount of time.

They earn points for every event in which they participate. At each event the students instantly receive an award, which proves that they participated. The participants challenge students from other classes during events. The common class/team goal is to get as many points as possible. The top-scoring team in each grade level can earn a party of some sort.

Meanwhile, the teachers are all together, seated at a table, recording the students' scores. They enjoy the time spent with other teachers and see the students enjoying themselves, without directly teaching them.

To be successful, the students have to move quickly, on their own, between events! They need to compete in every event in order to get the most points. They can double-check with their teacher to see which events they still have to visit. This is a great way to get the students to work up a sweat. The excitement and motivation to win make this very enjoyable.

Option 2 Guidelines

- If you have 15 classes coming out to compete at once, have approximately 17 events. Spread them out as far as you can.
- A good time frame is two hours.
- You'll need at least 17 volunteers.
- Start and stop on your signal.
- Award students who accomplish all events within the given time.

Field Day Themes

- "Olympics"
  - 50-yard dash
  - Hurdles
  - Long jump
  - Triple jump
  - Javelin
  - Basketball shooting
  - Softball pitching
  - Tennis serving
  - Gymnastics skills in an obstacle tumbling course
  - Relays
  - Silly relays

Wrestling with a cage ball. This is done in a sumo wrestling format, with the two participants trying to force each other out of the ring. Instead of pushing against each other, though, they push a cage ball that sits between them.

Decathlon—10 fun activities put together into a race

Pass-the-torch relay

Medal tossing

Shot put

Discus

Olympic ring toss

Greek pizza toss. A pizza is made with Play-Doh and students toss it back and forth to a partner; the most tosses wins. Or a student self-tosses it, and a high toss wins.

- "Field Day at the Beach"

Baywatch lifeguard 50-yard dash to water

Sand castle building

Water balloon run

"Tacky tourist" attire relay—putting on and taking off strange tourist attire

Beach blanket bingo—bingo on a beach blanket or towel

Beach pail waterfall—using spoons to fill a beach pail, the first pail to overflow wins, or the most water wins

Sand demand—a relay of filling a beach pail with sand, with the most sand winning

Surfing—imitating a surfer catching a wave

Beach volleyball

Beach ball fling

Beach ball basketball—using a Hula Hoop as a goal

Paddleball volleying—seeing how long one can paddle the ball before it gets out of control

Frisbee toss

Beach towel flicking—using a towel, flicking items down

Beach burying—five items thoroughly buried in sand as quickly as possible

Sun protection relay—collecting five protective items for one's team: sunscreen, hat, sunglasses, umbrella, and water bottle

Baywatch rescue relay—using a rescue tube or can and running to save one's teammates, who must be attached to the rescue apparatus at all times

Beach blanket bounce—racing to the finish line by stepping on a blanket only, not the ground

- Hawaiian

    Limbo

    "Hawaii Five-0" scooter race

    Lei around the cone

    Hula Hoop contest

    Pineapple and coconut relay. The first person in a group of six passes the pineapple through the legs of each player on the team, and the last person runs to the front and passes the coconut over the heads. The first group to get the coconut to the end wins.

- Country and Western

    Lasso the cone

    Ride-the-horse relay—climbing on the back of someone who's on all fours and doing a 30-foot race to the finish, using mats

    Line dancing

    Climb the rope

    Cowboy clothing relay—racing to the hat, to the belt, to the boots, and to the shirt, making sure they are all on and not being held by the hands in order to win

SPECIAL PHYSICAL EDUCATION DAYS

Kids are talking about it during lunch, in the hallways, and at home: the special days designed by the teachers in order to promote physical education. They are fun to plan, promote, and put on. When kids get excited about physical education, we are doing our job as teachers.

Obstacle

Choosing the appropriate special physical education days for your situation.

Common Mistakes

- Not doing anything extra.
- Thinking your job isn't going to require any thinking and work beyond the six-hour teaching day. If that is the case, then maybe you should look for another field. The extra thinking, time, and energy spent on a special event to promote physical education is well worth it.

Solutions

- Start off by approaching your principal with an idea for two events (one in the fall and one in the spring) to promote your program.
- Decide which ones you want to do and have fun with them.
- Include letters to parents, posters, and verbal announcements, and even use local media such as the newspaper and radio and TV stations to let everyone in the community know and get involved.
- Here are some fun ideas:

  Turkey Trot (one-mile run before Thanksgiving)

  Splash into Summer (water balloons, water limbo, greased watermelon, firefighter's relay)

  Jingle Bell Jog (one-mile run before Christmas)

  January Jump Shots (shooting baskets for time)

  Jump Rope for Heart (raises money for American Heart Association)

March Madness (basketball activities)

Spring Sprints (short races)

Fall Frolic (fun locomotor movement races)

Dance-a-thons

Olympics

Tips

- If you get the support of your principal, you can do all kinds of fun things to promote physical education.
- Try not to interrupt too much instruction time—do some events after school or on Saturdays.

Real-Life Story

Every special event that Ms. Sanders did was successful, because she was excited about the events. Her excitement rubbed off on the students. Each year the excitement grew and the events got better and better!

PICTURE DAY

Frilly dresses, high heels, sandals, ties, and other "no-no's" for physical education class all will surface on one inescapable day: picture day. Remember your mother or father saying, "Don't get dirty, don't mess up your hair, and smile pretty"?

This is school tradition. Wouldn't you hate to have a vigorous physical education class outside in the 90-degree heat, and then have spaghetti for lunch, on your picture day? If you thought the fancy outfits and trying not to get messed up on picture day were bad, what if you had to be in charge of picture day? They put all the cameras in the gym and schedule the students to get their photographs taken during physical education class at Dutch Elementary School.

Obstacle

Overcoming the dreaded picture day problems.

Common Mistakes

- Getting angry at the students who don't want to participate while they are in their picture-taking clothes.
- Forgetting what it is like to be a child on picture day.

Solutions

- Once you accept this as part of the school package and not fight it, you'll be OK.
- Do something that will make the day progress smoothly. Some ideas:

   Watch a video of the students during Field Day or during units in which you taped them.

   Organize a "dance show": "American Bandstand," "Soul Train," or "Club MTV." Ask students who are dressed up and looking and feeling good to be on the "show," and play different kinds of music while they are dancing so that they have to change their dance style: disco, funk, hard rock, metal, "elevator music," classical, country, punk, or alternative music. Encourage all the kids to dance while keeping them away from the dirt, grass, mud, and other outside elements.

   Show a sports "bloopers" video, but first preview it for acceptable content.

Tip

You are in a win-win situation. The students who hate missing physical education will only desire to have PE more! The ones who like to dance and see themselves and others on TV will enjoy watching the TV and dancing.

Real-Life Story

During picture day Ms. Stevens organized the "American Bandstand" activity. This involved students dancing to music on the stereo. There were 150 students in the gym, and all of them were glued to the activity. The next year, when picture day was approaching, the students asked to do "American Bandstand" again. They said it was "phat," or as Dick Clark might have said, "groovy."

OPEN HOUSE

You're having a party and you're all dressed up, and no one shows up. It's sad and pathetic, but it really happens.

The first week of school you meet and get to know the students. The second week, it's time to meet the parents and guardians of those students. The parents come to school ready to meet their child's new classroom teacher. The student is so excited to show off his desk and classroom. The teachers are on their best behavior and have on their best outfits, trying to make a good impression.

All teachers await the arrival of their guests with great anticipation. The physical education teachers are wearing dresses, hose, and high heels or suits and ties. They are waiting in the gym for the opportunity to brag about the students and the physical education program. They are waiting and waiting, and they will wait some more. Finally, a visitor walks through the hall and comes into the ignored gym. The child had to drag the parent to the gym. A few more students drag their parents to the gym. A total of 10 parents out of 800 show up at the gym that night. Do the parents not care about the physical education program? Do the students not care to take the time to introduce their parents to the physical education teachers?

Obstacle

Getting people to want to visit physical education during open house.

Common Mistake

Liking the solitude.

Solutions

- Conduct your physical education classes so that the parents want to visit the PE teachers because the students are talking so much about them.
- Play enticing, inviting music.
- Make your gym pleasing to the eye.
- In your newsletter, send home the dates and times of the open house and invite the families to visit you.

Tips

- Play the music loud enough to catch the attention of the parents as they wander through the hall.
- Talk to the students and tell them how much you want to meet their parents.

Real-Life Story

Knowing the typical pattern of the open house, the physical education teacher played the "Jock Jams" compact disc to attract the visitors to check out the gym. Like the Pied Piper, the parents followed the beat and the pleasing sound coming from the gym. They were drawn to something that caught their attention and brought their senses pleasure; just like physical education can do. Once you get the visitors in, you've got a captive audience to sell your program.

APPENDIX A

PHYSICAL EDUCATION PROVERBS AND SAYINGS

Students catch on to phrases that you use all the time. Sometimes they can even finish the sentences you start; then again, sometimes they can't. Here are examples of first-graders' interpretations of popular proverbs, phrases, and sayings:

A penny for your . . . lunch money.

All for one and one for . . . the money.

All good things must come . . . to time-out.

All work and no play makes John a . . . nerd.

All's well that ends . . . before it starts.

All's well that . . . paid the money.

Always lend a helping . . . of potatoes.

Be true to your . . . principal.

Birds of a feather . . . play badminton.

Count your . . . strikes.

Do unto others . . . if they hurt you first.

Don't kick a poor man . . . where it hurts.

Every dog has his . . . tail.

Get all your ducks . . . out of the pond.

Haste makes . . . a mess.

He's like a diamond in the . . . jewelry counter.

Honesty is the . . . way teachers force you to tell on yourself.

If at first you don't succeed . . . go back home.

If at first you don't succeed . . . quit.

If he jumps off a bridge . . . he'll die.

If I've said it once . . . I'm going to scream.

If you can't stand the heat . . . take off your clothes.

It's all in a day's . . . lunch.

It's better to have loved than . . . hate the other team.

Just because he did it, that doesn't mean you . . . didn't do it first.

Knock out two birds with one . . . gun.

Light as . . . sunshine.

Look what the cat . . . scratched.

Looking good is feeling . . . yourself.

Love, hope, and . . . crying.

Money doesn't . . . stay in my pocket.

Monkey see, monkey . . . sue.

No pain, . . . no aspirin.

Once is never . . . twice.

One bad apple . . . costs less.

One good turn deserves . . . at least a dollar.

One is the . . . winner.

People in glass houses . . . shouldn't do physical education.

Rain, rain, go . . . to God.

Slippery when . . . you don't have the right PE shoes.

Slowly, but . . . last.

Stop, look, and . . . *go!*

The early bird always gets . . . sleepy.

The early bird always gets . . . the blue light special.

The grass is not always greener . . . in Greenland.

There is no "I" in . . . PE.

There is no time like . . . the clock's.

There's no business like . . . minding your own.

Those who laugh last, laugh . . . loud.

Time heals all . . . bellyaches.

To be or . . . get in trouble.

Too many chiefs and not enough . . . makeup.

Too much of a good thing . . . means you always win.

Turn the other . . . kid around.

Two's company, three's . . . four.

When it rains, it . . . is time for video games.

When the going gets tough . . . run fast.

APPENDIX B

PHYSICAL EDUCATION DICTIONARY

This special dictionary is created from the words that students invent, thinking they are correct, and words that they think they understand but really don't:

aerobics—A language used in a faraway country. Also known as using oxygen to move during physical activity.

bolley—Also known as "volley."

cardiovascular—Spanish card game. Also known as the heart and vascular system.

crap—The painful ache you get at your side when you run. Also known as "cramp."

dribble—drool (first-graders); the way to handle the basketball with the eyes closed (fifth-grade boys).

endurance—The end of a dance. Also known as the ability to endure while exerting the body.

hyperextend—Get crazy or hyped up. Also known as extending beyond the natural, normal, comfortable position.

javelin—To run with the ball without dribbling in basketball. Also known as a long, thin implement used for throwing.

locomotor—A Ricky Martin song. Also known as the body moving in various ways.

obeast—An animal that's mean. Also known as "obese."

objective—Lawyers shout this in court. Also known as the goal that you try to reach each class.

out of balance—The boundary lines for games. Also known as "out of bounds."

penalty—A boy's private area. Also known as something negative, such as a point, that is given to a team that performs a violation or an illegality.

PE—Bubbly learning. Also known as "physical education."

shot put—A gun holder. Also known as a heavy piece of equipment that is thrown.

shredding—Keeping oneself afloat in deep water by sculling and kicking. Also known as treading water.

shuttlecock—Space center. Also known as a birdie or the object hit during a badminton game.

spike—A dog collar. Also known as an action used in volleyball to forcefully hit the ball over the net.

sprint—The people on the phone. Also known as a very fast run.

violation—A pretty color, or a little musical instrument. Also known as a penalty, or an infraction of rules.

FOR MORE INFORMATION

BIBLIOGRAPHY

Champion, W.T. 1990. *Fundamentals of Sports Law*. Deerfield, Ill., New York, and Rochester, N.Y.: Clark Boardman Callaghan.

Graham, G., S. Holt-Hale, and M. Parker. 1993. *Children Moving: A Reflective Approach to Teaching Physical Education*. 3d ed. Palo Alto, Calif.: Mayfield.

Lumpkin, Angela. 1986. *Physical Education: A Contemporary Introduction*. St. Louis: Times Mirror Mosby College Publishing.

National Association for Sport and Physical Education (NASPE). *Developmentally Appropriate Physical Education Practices for Children*. Champaign, Ill.: Human Kinetics Publishers.

Sherrill, Claudine. 1993. *Adapted Physical Activity Recreation and Sport*. 4th ed. Dubuque, Iowa: Brown & Benchmark Publishers.

Sizer, F.S., E.N. Whitney, and L.K. DeBruyne. 1994. *Making Life Choices: Health Skills and Concepts*. St. Paul, Minn.: West Publishing Co.

OTHER HELPFUL RESOURCES

Teaching Elementary Physical Education: The Independent Voice of Elementary and Middle School Physical Educators. Human Kinetics Publishing.

The Journal of Physical Education, Recreation & Dance (JOPERD). American Alliance for Health, Physical Education, Recreation and Dance.

Great Activities: A Newspaper For Elementary & Middle School Physical Education Teachers. Great Activities Publishing Co.

PHYSICAL EDUCATION ORGANIZATIONS AND WEB SITES

PE Central, **www.pecentral.org/**

PELinks4U, **www.pelinks4u.org/**

Human Kinetics, **www.humankinetics.com/**

Sportsmedia, **www.sports-media.org/**

President's Physical Fitness Challenge, **www.indiana.edu/ ~preschal**

The President's Council on Physical Fitness and Sport, **www.fitness.gov**

Concerned Adults and Students for Physical Education Reform (CASPER), **www.csuchico.edu/casper/about.html**

National Association for Health & Fitness, **www.physicalfitness.org/**

Project Fit America, **www.projectfitamerica.org/**

Spark, **www.foundation.sdsu.edu/projects/spark/index.html**

International Association for Sports Information, **http://sportquest.com/**

American Alliance of Health, Physical Education, Recreation & Dance (AAHPERD), **www.aahperd.org/**

State chapters of APHERD, **www.aahperd.org/**

National Association for Sport and Physical Education (NASPE), **www.aapherd.org/naspe/**

American Alliance for Active Lifestyles and Fitness, **www.aapherd.org/aaalf/**

PHYSICAL EDUCATION NEWSLETTERS

PELinks4U Newsletter, **www.pelinks4u.org/**
PE Central Newsletter, **www.pecentral.org/**
UPDATE, **www.aapherd.org/**

ABOUT THE AUTHOR

Charmain Sutherland is a physical education specialist at Holland Elementary School in Virginia Beach, Virginia, who has worked in private and public schools for more than a decade. She has taught physical education and health to every type of student—at-risk, disadvantaged, and privileged—and has coached a variety of sports. In April 2001, Charmain received a national teaching award presented by Coca-Cola and Healthsouth for developing a dynamic physical education program that exceeded the expectations of her city, state, and school. A member of the American Alliance for Health, Physical Education, Recreation and Dance, she is a popular speaker at state conventions and citywide in-services in Virginia Beach. Charmain earned a master's degree in physical education, administration, and supervision from Old Dominion University.